# Balancing the Generations

## A Leader's Guide to the Complex, Multi-Generational, 21st Century Workplace

Bob Mason

ISBN: 978-1-61434-227-4
LCCN: 2011926807

Published in the United States by Palmarium Publishing, Albuquerque, New Mexico.

Cover Design by Todd Engel

Printed in the United States of America on acid-free paper.

For more information about the content of this book, contact RLM Planning and Leadership at rlm@planleadexcel.com

First Edition

# Balancing the Generations

A Leader's Guide to the Complex, Multi-Generational, 21st Century Workplace

Bob Mason

**Palmarium Publishing**
Albuquerque, NM

# Acknowledgements

A book such as this is the result of contributions from many people. Generations in the workplace is a topic that never fails to start a discussion and, although they too far numerous to mention, I extend my sincere appreciation to all who contributed stories, examples, ideas, and suggestions to make this book more complete. Their contributions sometimes validated my own thinking but also often caused me to take another look at what I thought was true.

There are a few people whose contributions were especially noteworthy and who helped me put it all together.

Vicki Clark at Clarkson University planted the seed that has grown into this book and for that I am very grateful.

Angela Hoy at Booklocker helped me through the process of getting this book published. She was always very patient, answering all my questions, no matter how mundane they may have seemed to her.

Sharon Jeffers did an outstanding job editing; correcting my many errors and suggesting more appropriate usage and arrangement of the language. Any errors still in the text are because of my mistakes in making corrections.

For the last 29 years, my strongest support has always come from my wife, Wanda. She made many valuable suggestions for the book and provided encouragement when it didn't look like I'd ever finish.

# Table of Contents

INTRODUCTION......................................................................1
PART I...................................................................................9
    CHAPTER 1 – DEFINING THE GENERATIONS............................ 11
    CHAPTER 2 – DEPRESSION, WARS, AND STARTING OVER:
    THE GI AND SILENT GENERATIONS...................................... 20
    The GI Generation............................................................ 20
    The Silent Generation...................................................... 26
    CHAPTER 3 – THE BABY BOOM GENERATION ........................ 33
    CHAPTER 4 – GENERATION X AND THE MILLENNIALS .............. 52
    Generation X ................................................................... 52
    The Millennials................................................................ 63
    CHAPTER 5 – GENDER ISSUES AND IMMIGRANTS IN THE
    WORKPLACE.................................................................... 71
    Gender Issues.................................................................. 71
    Immigration ..................................................................... 76
    CHAPTER 6 – BUT THAT ISN'T ME! THOSE WHO DON'T FIT.... 79

PART II ................................................................................83
    CHAPTER 7 – LEADING THE GENERATIONS ........................... 85
    CHAPTER 8 – WHAT YOU WANT IS NOT WHAT I NEED ............ 89
    CHAPTER 9 – HOW DO I MOTIVATE THEE LET ME
    DISCOVER THE WAYS ...................................................... 102
    CHAPTER 10 – I KNOW YOU HEARD WHAT YOU THINK I
    SAID BUT DID I SAY WHAT YOU THINK YOU HEARD? ....... 114
    CHAPTER 11 – IT TAKES ALL KINDS GENERATIONS AND
    DIVERSITY IN THE WORKPLACE ........................................ 122
    CHAPTER 12 – WHY SHOULD I CHANGE? WHY CAN'T YOU
    CHANGE?...................................................................... 128
    CHAPTER 13 – HOW DO I KEEP THEM FROM LEAVING?........ 141
    CHAPTER 14 – WHAT DOES THE FUTURE HOLD AND WHAT
    CAN I DO ABOUT IT?...................................................... 148

*Bob Mason*

APPENDIX A – THE TIMELINE OF GENERATIONS ..................... 161
APPENDIX B – BRIEF FACTS ABOUT THE GENERATIONS ......... 163
NOTES ............................................................................... 167

# Introduction

Throughout my professional life, I've had the privilege of leading thousands of people covering five generations. Through the years, I've noticed not only the differences in various age groups, which we like to neatly group into generations, but also the interesting, and sometimes contentious ways the various generations interact with each other.

As a student of leadership, I've found this generational conflict to be not only an interesting subject to study, but also a critical aspect of the leadership challenge. Whereas leaders of 50 or even 20 years ago did not spend much time worrying about how to incorporate various generations into a cohesive workplace, today's leader must juggle the significant differences of four sometimes seemingly diametrically opposed generations. Senior corporate leaders find it difficult to comprehend young people who don't understand or want to follow the rules, written and unwritten, while young leaders can't seem to understand why their seniors have so many rules in the first place.

This book first explores each generation, examining the influences that acted on them, especially in their formative years, and the significant national events that shaped that generation as a whole. To complicate matters, there is some disagreement on what periods actually define each generation. I don't wish to enter that fray, as my goal is to provide a look at the various generations and how leaders might better lead their members. In fact, generations are sometimes defined more by national or world events than specific dates, so I will use generally accepted periods. I understand that some may disagree, but ask that readers not become mired in those details which are not terribly significant to the mission of this book.

The naming of the generations is also somewhat imprecise and there is disagreement among writers and commentators. As with the argument for specific dates, naming of generations is not critical, so for this book I've chosen to use what I found to be the most common moniker associated with each generation. There is one exception which I'll discuss shortly.

The second part of the book is dedicated to suggestions for the leader to effectively use this information and navigate the often complex issues that accompany today's multi-generational workplace. You may be tempted to skip directly to Part II if you're in a hurry, but please take the time to read Part I because it provides the foundation for the suggestions in the second part.

In researching this subject, I concentrated on U.S. history and the American definition of terms. Especially when discussing earlier generations, it is common to find different definitions, and even time periods, among European writers reflecting the difference in experiences and, to some degree, in language. Though significant with earlier generations, this difference seems to become less so when referring to more modern times; a consequence of our completely connected world. My purpose is to provide a background of events that occurred during those specific time periods rather than to provide a comprehensive review of U.S. history and so the text cites only some of the more significant historical events which occurred during each of the generations.

As you read, you'll most likely think of events you feel were significant but are not mentioned. People view history through the lens of their own experience. What may be significant to one person or group of people might seem less important to others, so I may not discuss something that you feel is important; perhaps some defining moment you experienced or a national event that has changed your life. Such possible exclusions illustrate a critical point that you will see repeated throughout this book; that each person approaches life from a specific set of personal experiences, upbringing, and learning. Though it is convenient to group people into generational categories, each one of us is an individual and will not always fit when lumped into a generalized category with millions of others.

In researching this book, I often found that sometimes the commonly accepted view of different generations and the events associated with them were not always consistent with the facts. For instance, the Baby Boom generation gets much of the credit, or blame, for the unrest which occurred in the 1960s and 1970s. While many Boomers certainly took part in protests and rallies, there's a little more to the story. The reality in such cases is important to understanding the generations. I also found that much of the literature about a certain generation was written by someone from that generation, sometimes seemingly with an axe to grind.

As you read these pages, you will be tempted to apply your own experiences and memories, especially when reading about your own generation. It's completely normal to inject your own experiences, and even prejudice, into any discussion of generations; but, as I have tried to keep my own from these pages, or at least identify them, you must do the same in order to truly gain the understanding necessary to be an effective leader in a multi-generational environment. Always keep in mind that your memories of events, shaped by your own experience and upbringing, may be different than that of others.

In order to understand how to lead people of different age groups, it's important to know a little about them. It has become common to categorize people into the various generations and use those categories to define the people in that age group. Though it's a mistake to lump everyone together without considering the individual, it is helpful to understand a little about the different generations and the unique challenges each has experienced.

Generations are large periods, so researchers further break them into cohorts to describe groups based on birth years within the overall generation. Though generations do have some commonality, there can be big differences between the cohorts. For instance, later cohorts of the Silent Generation will have different memories and impressions of the depression era than those in an earlier cohort. [1]

The first generation we'll discuss is the GI Generation covering those born between about 1900 and 1927. There are still a few members of this generation in the workforce today. Even more significant is that this generation includes many very wealthy business owners. A review of the Forbes 400 list of the 400 richest people in America reveals a large percentage of GI Generation members.[2] There is another reason to understand this group. In many ways, each generation affects the following generation and that is especially true in this case as during their lifetime these people experienced economic boom, the great depression, and World War II. These experiences shaped a very patriotic group of people who were also quite cautious in the way they managed personal finances. Their influence can definitely be seen in the next two generations.

Labeling of generational categories is not an exact science. Different researchers and authors have developed different generational nomenclature. For this book, I will attempt to use the most common names for generations. I make one exception. What I and other authors call the GI Generation is often referred to as The Greatest Generation, a term coined by TV anchorman Tom Brokaw in his book by the same name. While the title certainly sold books, it also raised a lot of discontent among other generations. My purpose is not to pit one group against another and I feel the term GI Generation is more accurate, so that is how I will refer to that group.

People born between about 1927 and 1945 are generally classified as the Silent Generation. Stuck between the GI Generation and the Baby Boomers, this category is often forgotten. In fact, not everyone breaks out this generation, instead including them as later cohorts of the GI Generation and sometimes referring to the whole group as Traditionalists. I address them separately because they are an important group, and had a significant, distinct role in the later Baby Boomer Generation. This generation is the only one for which I do use a specific date; 1927. That date is important because a person born then turned 18 in 1945 and the vast majority of its members were too young to serve in World War II.

Probably the best known category is the Baby Boom generation. This is the group born between 1945 and approximately 1964. Recent work by Jonathan Pontell suggests breaking the baby boom generation at about 1954 into a new category. That category, which he identifies as Generation Jones, includes those born between 1954 and 1965. While Pontell makes interesting points, I have not found sufficient reason to split this group out of the Baby Boomer Generation as I will discuss in more detail later.

Generation X comprises those born between the mid 1960s and the late 1970s. This is, demographically, the smallest group but they are having a large impact on the workplace. They are somewhat unique in that they're sandwiched between two very large generational groups.

The Millennial Generation, sometimes called Generation Y, covers the period between the end of Generation X and the early 2000s. This group is the largest generation yet and its members are beginning to become more prominent in the workplace as the youngest members attain working age.

As you read about the different generations, notice that while they are different, they also have many similarities. Also, note the sometimes very significant impact one generation has on another. Often, what one generation is blamed for or credited with is really the result of actions by members of a previous generation. Finally, it can't be overemphasized that each generation is composed of individuals, each with different experiences. While the various generations tend to show general homogeneity, some more than others, they are still made up of people who may or may not think like the group.

# PART I

# Chapter 1
# Defining the Generations

"You just don't understand!" "This generation just doesn't get it!" Just about everyone has heard those comments and has probably uttered something similar. They may well have been right as people of different ages have experienced different lives, with different experiences. What may be clear to someone who is 18 years old may not be as clear to someone who is 40 years old: and vice versa. This is commonly referred to as the generation gap and it is very real. Leaders now have to deal with four different generations in the workplace and that isn't easy. To best meet this challenge, a leader must first understand a little about the different generations; their experiences, how they see the world, and what motivates them.

Humans love to categorize. We are happiest when we can put everything in nice neat packages. Sometimes we'll even invent a new group just to prevent something or someone from appearing out of place. In our penchant for order we do not exclude ourselves. We place people in categories and call them generations. These generational groupings have gone well beyond just a way to neatly order ourselves, and have become a pre-judgment of what people are and what they may or may not do. Careful study of the generations provides useful clues to potential behavior, but they are only clues. These generational groupings are made up of individuals and individuals act - individually. As the saying goes, no two people are alike. So, maybe you just don't understand, but it will help you as a leader to get an idea what your subordinates may be thinking based on what they have experienced. This is not an exact science! Far from it. In fact, generational categories are only one of many things a leader needs to consider.

So if everyone is different, what good are these categories? Do they have any real use for an organization's leader? I believe they do, but only when applied carefully and with more than just anecdotal information. Like all things, the more you know the more effective you'll be. Therefore, it's important to understand the general experiences that provide the prism through which the different generations see the world. As humans, our attitudes, values, as well as our outlook are generally formed in the first years of our lives and so what was going on around us then has a significant impact on what we will become. That isn't to say we don't change as we grow and have new experiences, or that world changes won't lead us to modify our basic beliefs.

Unfortunately, the tendency is to lump everyone into those nice neat boxes we call generations, and that's where the leader can make a grave error. That nice neat box is usually pretty big. What is true at one end of the box may not be so true at the other end. The Baby Boom Generation is a great example of that. The world immediately following World War II and the world of the early 1960s, generally accepted as the boundaries of the Baby Boom Generation, were two very different periods making it very difficult to succinctly categorize all baby boomers. In fact, one commentator has proposed carving a new generational category from the late Baby Boomer generation: more on that later. Likewise, the Millennial Generation is divided by the events of September 11, 2001. In fact, those events may have had a lasting effect on people of previous generations as well.

Before we proceed, two important questions beg to be answered. First, what exactly is a generation? The New World Dictionary defines a generation as "the average period (about thirty years) between the birth of one generation and that of the next." A subsequent definition states, "A group of such people with some experience, belief, attitude, etc, in common." As commonly defined, generational groupings cover a period of less than 30 years and so the second definition is more appropriate. We will be discussing groups of people who have generally had the same experience and in many cases have developed some of the same beliefs and attitudes.

The second and certainly more complex question is in two parts. How are people influenced by events that occur in their lifetimes, and when do these influences occur? This is the subject of considerable study in the fields of psychology and sociology, but a detailed review of human development is beyond the scope of this book. It is beneficial though for the leader to at least have a basic understanding of the subject. For that, we turn to the work of Erik Erickson who defined eight stages of development through which he believed a normal human will progress. Each stage presents new challenges and each hopefully builds on the previous stage.[1]

The first two stages are Infancy, 0-1 years, and Toddler, 2-3 years. Development during these stages is primarily centered on the parent or primary caregiver and concentrates on the child's development of trust and autonomy. It is during the toddler stage that the child begins to develop confidence in his or her own ability. [2] Though parent or caregiver actions are critical at this stage, it is too early to develop the generational beliefs and attitudes that are our subject.

The next stage, Pre-school, covers years 4 through 6 and is concerned with initiative and feelings of guilt. Erickson feels that this stage is where a child begins to want to accomplish his or her own actions for a reason. They begin to feel a new emotion; guilt. This conflict between initiative and guilt presents a challenge to the child. He or she may engage in risk-taking behavior or behavior that is considered inappropriate like yelling or hitting. Pre-school children are more able to accomplish tasks on their own and how the parent or caregiver react to this is critical in their development. Children who are encouraged at this stage will develop initiative and independence. Those who aren't will be more likely to develop guilt about their own needs and desires.[3]

I believe this is a critical period in a child's development as they begin to learn about making choices and become aware of their own thoughts and ideas. They also begin to be aware of others and the world around them and while children at this stage aren't ready to adopt the societal beliefs and attitudes of the day, they are definitely beginning to pick up on the values of the parents or caregiver. This may have a significant impact on how, or how much they later adopt those beliefs and attitudes.

The next stage, Childhood, is ages 7 to 12 years which Erickson identifies as Industry vs. Inferiority. Erickson states that at this stage children become more aware of themselves as individuals and that this is a critical time for development of their self-confidence. He says "Ideally, elementary school provides many opportunities for children to achieve the recognition of teachers, parents and peers by producing things - drawing pictures, solving addition problems, writing sentences, and so on. If children are encouraged to make and do things and are then praised for their accomplishments, they begin to demonstrate industry by being diligent, persevering at tasks until completed and putting work before pleasure." Most importantly for our study, this is the age when children begin to form moral values and recognize differences in people and cultures.[4]

Therefore, I see this as the time when children really begin to be affected, on a personal level, by the larger society and when they begin to develop generational beliefs and attitudes. Again though, notice the continued critical impact on the parent or caregiver.

Erickson's next stage, Adolescence covers the years 13 - 19. He calls this period identity vs. role confusion. At this stage the teenager (not really a child anymore) begins to have concerns about how they appear to others. Belonging to something becomes important as the teenager begins to develop an identity that is part of something else such as school or a job.[5] This is also an important period for our purposes as it is this period where young people really begin to develop the beliefs and attitudes associated with others in their generation.

The sixth stage is Young Adulthood, 20 to 34 years. Erickson labels this Intimacy vs. Isolation. This is a time when young adults still want to fit in with friends and are often afraid of rejection. Erickson states that "Once people have established their identities, they are ready to make long-term commitments to others. They become capable of forming intimate, reciprocal relationships (e.g. through close friendships or marriage) and willingly make the sacrifices and compromises that such relationships require."[6] I believe this is also a significant developmental period. Though we categorize generations by dates, they tend to overlap some and it is at this age that young people really begin to interact, on a mature and often professional level, with people from the previous generations. How they interact has changed as we shall see later.

The last two stages, Middle Adulthood: Generativity vs. Stagnation (35 to 65 years), and Senior: Integrity vs. Despair (65 years onwards), involve contributing to society, teaching the next generation and reviewing life's successes and failures.[7] This doesn't mean that learning is over or that beliefs can't change. However, it is uncommon for people in these last two categories to change those beliefs and attitudes developed in their younger years, though those beliefs and attitudes may mellow in fervor.

Erickson's categories show us that we develop our basic belief structure at a fairly young age and that future stages of our lives are then based on those early lessons. That's why, when looking at the generations as a leader, it's very helpful to know a little about where people come from and what they experienced during those formative years. When considering the impact of events on development of the different generations, it is vital one doesn't overlook the experiences of the preceding generation. As Erickson's work shows, a developing child relies very heavily on the influence of a parent/primary caregiver throughout most of the developmental years. While the events of his or her generation have a great impact on the members of that generation, it is the influence of the parent/primary caregiver that will most often determine how the individual members of the generation react to those events. That is probably one of the most difficult aspects of leading different generations: as a leader, you will probably never know the influences that acted on a particular person during those formative years.

Location can have a big effect during a person's formative years. I spent my junior high and the first year and a half of high school in large urban schools. My family moved while I was a sophomore and I completed high school in a small school in a very small Midwestern town. The atmosphere was completely different as were beliefs and attitudes. As I will discuss in Part II, this location differential can result in significant differences even within a generational group. Among earlier generations location could have an even greater impact as there was not the connectivity available today. Small town America did not have the same access to information as the larger, metropolitan areas. That difference has been largely erased by the far-reaching internet; however, there is still great disparity in the availability of high speed internet access between urban and rural areas of the country.

Likewise, the influence of parents, relatives, and others close to a young child in the first stages of life will have an extremely significant influence on how they interact with their own generation and how much they internalize the attitudes and beliefs of that generation.

As I mentioned before, each person has different influences in their lives and so simply being a member of a specific generation does not neatly define them. In their study of life course theory, Johnson and Crosnoehave identified five general principles.

1. The Principle of Life-Span Development: Human development and aging are lifelong processes.

2. The Principle of Agency: Individuals construct their own life course through the choices and actions they take within the opportunities and constraints of history and social circumstance.

3. The Principle of Time and Place: The life course of individuals is embedded and shaped by the historical times and places they experience over their lifetime.

4. The Principle of Timing: The developmental antecedents and consequences of life transitions, events and behavioral patterns vary according to their timing in a person's life.

5. The Principle of Linked Lives: Lives are lived interdependently and socio-historical influences are expressed through this network of shared relationships.[8]

These five principles very accurately describe the various types of influences that act on all people. Again, it's essential for a leader to understand that they most likely will not know how the majority of these principles have influenced their subordinates.

A discussion with a teacher with 25 years of classroom experience illustrates the point. Part way through his career he moved from a school in a lower class neighborhood to one in an upper middle class neighborhood. He said the difference in the student's approach to learning was striking. These students were in the same generational group, yet those in the lower class neighborhood were much more willing to accept failure. Their lives, in general, had not been the picture of success. He found that even small victories had a profound effect on their ability to succeed. Conversely, the students from the upper middle class neighborhoods didn't expect failure, and so had a harder time dealing with it. They also required a bigger success before they were impressed. They saw those same small victories as just something that was supposed to happen.

This teacher also didn't feel that, at least at the elementary school level, the more or less arbitrary categorization of students by birth year was really appropriate. In fact, he didn't really see a big difference through the years in behavior or motivation. He did comment though that the tendency for today's students to be more tech savvy is evident, commenting that shy students will now text him questions in contrast to a previous time when they would just keep those questions to themselves.

# Chapter 2

# Depression, Wars, and Starting Over:
# The GI and Silent Generations

## The GI Generation

The 1920s was an exciting time in the United States. With the end of World War I, the country had successfully flexed its muscle on the international stage and secured a position as a power to be reckoned with. World War I was billed as "the war to end all wars" and many Americans expected that the world was entering a period of permanent peace among nations. Though the years immediately following World War I were not particularly prosperous, by about 1921, the country was enjoying an economic boom. Older members of the GI Generation were in their twenties, enjoying affluence in the prime of their lives.

What is sometimes forgotten about the GI Generation is that they also experienced a boom in technology that is in some ways comparable to that of the late twentieth century. From 1900 to the 1950s the automobile, radio, television, the airplane, and penicillin, all became part of American life.

From about 1921 to 1928, most segments of America enjoyed an unprecedented economic boom. The boom didn't last though and the economy started to collapse in 1928; in what would become one of the most significant events of this generation.

Even today, economists debate the causes of the great depression. Several economic conditions and missteps occurred and by the late 1920s they would combine to cause an economic catastrophe. American farmers suffered a down turn after World War I when European's were able to return to farming, thus reducing the overseas markets for American agricultural goods and driving down profits. At the same time, government actions, especially a tightening of the money supply by the Fed worked to cause a period of deflation. On Wall Street, concerns with government actions, specifically new tariffs on imported goods, coupled with a rapid sell-off by stock speculators resulted in the stock market loosing 40% of its value in one day.[1]

Concurrently, banks in the Midwest, affected by the farm failures, began to close, taking even more money out of the system. Though these failures were little noticed at first, it wasn't long before the general public lost trust in banks and, when they saw the larger ones begin to fail, pulled their money from their own banks. In 1930, this "run" on the banks caused even more to fail.[2] Economic disaster had arrived.

As the recession turned into a full-blown depression, nature intervened to make the situation much worse for Midwestern America. Beginning in 1930 and lasting for about 10 years, severe drought and poor farming methods caused catastrophic soil loss. Dry winds resulted in what was termed "the dustbowl". Farmers who were already suffering found farming impossible.

So why study a generation that is not part of the work force? As noted before, there are still members of the GI Generation who own large corporations, but more importantly, the GI Generation had a profound impact on the generations to follow. The two biggest events of their time, the depression and World War II, left an indelible impression which they passed on to future generations and set the course for the next 80 years.

During the great depression, America suffered tremendous unemployment. In the ten years from 1923 to 1933, unemployment went from 3.3% to 24.9%.[3] A full quarter of those eligible to work had no job and no income. The pictures of men at soup kitchens and standing in bread lines are seared into our national history. Often ignored in discussion of the depression is that, at least for the earlier cohorts of the generation, these hard times followed a period of great prosperity, making recession and depression even more of a shock!

The depression would not end until the beginning of World War II. So, the GI generation went from boom to bust to war. Between 1941 and 1945, over 16 million Americans served in the armed forces and over 405,000 died.[4] By 1945, the U.S. population was almost 140 million[5] of which over 28 million were male between the ages of 18 and 44.[6] That means there was almost no one who wasn't touched by the war. These figures also indicate a big change ushered in by the GI Generation. As the numbers show, a huge portion of the male work force had gone to war. At the same time, industrial production would vastly increase to meet the war demands. With the male working population decimated, women began working in large numbers in what had been traditionally male jobs. Known collectively as "Rosie the Riveter," these women built ships, tanks, airplanes, and numerous other products needed by the war effort. Prior to the war, only about 25% of the female population was employed.[7] Women who did work were in traditionally female jobs such as secretaries and teachers. As more and more men joined the military the nation's workforce shrunk to a level insufficient for the vast increase in industrial capacity necessary for the war effort. A concerted effort was launched to recruit women to fill the jobs - and the women responded. Most worked because of a feeling of patriotism and a desire to help, but the lure of industrial jobs that paid well was also a draw. By 1945, an additional 6.5 million women had joined the work force, and approximately 2.5 million of those were employed in industrial or factory type work.[8] When the war was over, these women were often unceremoniously cashiered and sent home to be homemakers once again. Some were fine with that, but a large number were not. They had tasted independence and found it suited them.[9]

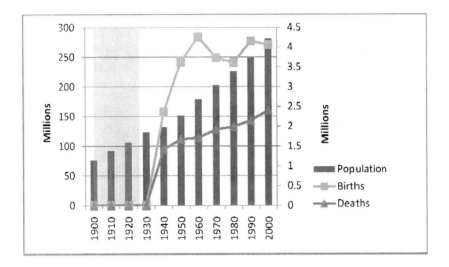

Figure 1.

GI Generation population, births and deaths [10]

Teamwork and collective effort seem to be a hallmark of the GI Generation. Their military experience taught them to work together in teams with definite hierarchical structure. In their book, *Generations: The History of America's Future 1584 to 2069*, Strauss and Howe comment that this generation is the most uniformed in history. From the forest green dress of the Civilian Conservation Corps, to the various scouting organizations which became popular at the time, to the military, GIs were predominantly in groups and organizations.[11]

Victorious in World War II, the GI Generation is accustomed to success. The generation boasts seven U.S. presidents and more than 100 Nobel Prize winners. But most importantly, the generation is used to getting its collective way. Such initiatives as age discrimination laws and a decrease in the eligibility age for social security happened just in time to benefit the GIs.[12] As a product of the post-depression expansion of government services, and their own tendency to work in groups and teams, the generation relies more and more on what the government does for them. Programs such as Social Security, created when they were young, assure them the government will always be there to help. At the height of their political power, GIs enacted Medicare, another program to provide government support to the populace.

The GI generation was also significantly healthier than the preceding generations, with infant mortality falling by 50% and life expectancy to age 65 rising by 20%. They also became more educated with average length of schooling rising from 9th to 12th grade and the number of 20-year olds in college increasing three-fold.[13] The post-war GI Bill provided generous educational benefits which were eagerly utilized by many who were returning from the war.

An area where the GI Generation was certainly not at the cutting edge is computer technology. Though much early development of computers was accomplished by this generation, it would be the following generations that led the way in making computer technology an almost indispensible part of human life. Some members of the GI Generation were quick to adapt and embraced the possibilities this new technology offered, but for many, computers represented a technology that was a little beyond their capability to adapt.

Though it is difficult to define, there was a significant change to this generation during the early post-war years; about 1945 to 1950. As noted a large portion of the population had gone off to war and then returned to a country that had changed. Many more women were working, the depression was over, but there was a typical post-war recession. The war had motivated many to reach new heights and in some ways break free of their previous lives. One indication of this desire to strike out anew is the divorce rate. The divorce rate between 1943 and 1950 soared, reaching 4.3 per 1000 in 1946, a figure that would not be reached again for another 27 years.[14] During this period child rearing techniques would also change, at least for some. We'll see that more in the next chapter.

In spite of computers, this generation truly led the way to a new America. Though often lost in the middle, there was another generational grouping between the GIs and the Boomers. These were people who were born a little too late to have been in World War II but were not quite Baby Boomers.


## The Silent Generation

The Silent Generation is generally considered those born between about 1927 and 1945. In their youth, this generation watched their parents endure the depression and then saw their fathers and older brothers march off to war. The older members of this generation were in their teens when the depression ended, and saw the effect on their parents and relatives. The youngest members were born after the depression had generally run its course and been alleviated by war-time production, but they learned of the hard times from parents, siblings, and relatives and most have no less of a vivid reaction to those years. An important footnote to this generation is that they are very familiar with the hard times of the depression, but did not experience the boom times immediately preceding it.

This generation also watched as their mothers went off to work in the factories. They became the first generation of children who very likely did not have at least one parent at home all the time. Almost all Silent Generation members were too young to have been sent to war, just barely, and many felt they had not had the opportunity to serve.

That opportunity would soon come for many. The Korean War, between 1950 and 1953 served to combine these generations somewhat. After World War II, the U.S. drastically reduced the size of the military and by 1950 there were less than 1.5 million Americans in uniform. By 1953, military end strength was at 3.6 million. [15] Recognizing the need to rapidly expand the military to meet the threat in Korea, the government began drafting World War II veterans as well as members of the Silent Generation who had been too young for that war. For those who served at that time the Korean War may have provided some unity of the two generations; however, the public reaction to the war was considerably different. While World War II was a clear victory, the Korean War ended in a truce, with no victory or clear cut outcome. It is not celebrated as a great American endeavor; in fact The Korean War is often called the forgotten war adding to the feeling that the Silent Generation was not well recognized as a separate group. Interestingly, a Korean War memorial was dedicated in Washington D.C. in 1995, nine years before the World War II memorial would be completed.

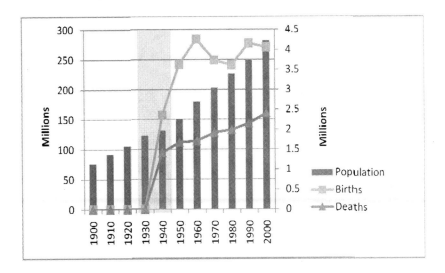

Figure 2.

Silent Generation population, births and deaths [16]

The Silent Generation found itself between two strong and much larger groups; the GI Generation and the Baby Boomers. They were raised by a very child protecting society but didn't really feel a part of anything. While the GI Generation tended to be carried along by the events of the day; boom, then depression, then world war, the Silent Generation experienced much of that second hand. In their younger years they tended to be a little rebellious, but in a respectful way. As they grew older though, they began to see that there was room for improvement in

American society. Many consider the Silent Generation to be something of a second string to the GI Generation and somewhat Baby Boomer want-to-be's. Strauss and Howe opine that the Silent Generation never really attained leadership, but were simply commentators on the world situation and seconds to those leaders from other generations. They point out that this generation, unlike the GIs and Boomers, did not produce a single president, though Presidents Jimmy Carter and George H.W. Bush were close; both being born in 1924.[17] It's significant to note however; that while development of the space program began with the GI generation, it was the Silent Generation's Neil Armstrong and Buzz Aldrin who set foot on the moon.

That the Silent Generation didn't produce leaders is a little incorrect. While it's true, there are no Silent Generation presidents, there certainly were leaders to emerge from the generation, as its members began to seriously question policies of racial discrimination, women's rights, and other social issues. Dr. Martin Luther King, born in 1929, led what would become a national civil rights movement that included both black and white followers and would extend well into following generations. Cesar Chavez, born 1927, led a movement to improve working conditions for migrant farm workers and founded the United Farm Workers union.[18] Women's rights leaders such as Betty Friedan, born 1921, took on a leadership role in a movement that had started in the 19th century. The movement began to take center stage as women sought to throw off the traditional domestic roles and become part of the mainstream American workforce. Also, the Silent Generation has the interesting distinction of driving the market in dietary aids, exercise classes, cosmetic surgery, and similar self-improvement or anti-aging products, as they try to return to their earlier years.[19]

The Silent generation did see its share of significant events. On October 4th, 1957, the Soviet Union launched the first satellite to orbit the Earth. Though hard to understand in this day of frequent manned space missions, this event shook America deeply and resulted in acceleration of America's own space program and the creation of the National Aeronautics and Space Administration, NASA.[20] They also watched as the threat of nuclear war became a fact of daily life and they learned to "duck and cover." Communism seemed to be sweeping the world and "the red scare" became a common topic, leading to congressional hearings and public hysteria.

America emerged from World War II with the strongest economy among the world's nations and after a normal post-war economic downturn, enjoyed a boom period of prosperity. The 1950s were prosperous but the 1960s were a period of huge economic growth, sometimes more than 6%.[21] Following the post-war period, the first recession was in the late 1960s, meaning the youngest members of the Silent Generation made it to adulthood with little or no economic troubles.

Just when the Silent Generation thought the world had settled down a little, the personal computer exploded onto the scene. This time, a group of Boomers would produce a revolution that affected everyone before and after their own generation. As computers became more common in the workplace and in homes across America, many in the Silent Generation did their best to adapt, many becoming quite knowledgeable and proficient. However, some saw the computer as something they could never really understand and found themselves in a sort of love-fear relationship. I know a Silent Generation couple who personifies this relationship. They have their own computer system set up in their home. They use it for such things as email and word processing; however, they have no idea how it works and even the slightest problem is cause to bring in an expert (at considerable expense) for consultation. They have become quite accustomed to having the technology available, but they continue to harbor a little fear because it is something they don't understand.

The GI and Silent Generations have one trait that I find unique among the generational categories. That is, no matter where in the country they originate, the social standing of their families, or the circumstances of their upbringing, they all share a common memory of depression and war. These two factors absolutely permeate their memories and whatever else they did for the rest of their lives; these two experiences are deeply imprinted in their psyche and will always color their outlook. I believe this is significant as both generations contributed to the Baby Boom generation, but more importantly set the tone for post-war America well into the next 40 years. I find no other generation that affected their own future as much. Some may disagree and point out the great social shift occurring during the Baby Boom years, but as I'll show in the next chapter, that shift was largely led by members of the Silent, and to a lesser extent, the GI Generation.

# Chapter 3
# The Baby Boom Generation

It was the 15th of August, 1969, in a field on Max Yasgur's dairy farm near Bethel, New York. Five hundred thousand people filled the field over the next three days for a music festival that would come to be known simply as Woodstock. It was to become the iconic event of the Baby Boom Generation.

The Baby Boom generation includes those born from about 1945 to 1964. Various authors put the end date for this generation anywhere from 1959 to 1964. In fact, Jonathan Pontell ends the Baby Boom Generation at 1954 and includes a separate generation group from 1954 to 1965.[22] For this study, we'll use the traditional Baby Boom years but will discuss the concept of a separate generation for late Boomers.

Appropriately enough, the Baby Boom Generation is named for the fact that the end of World War II brought on the largest birth rate in American history. The birth rate in 1945 was approximately 2.8 per thousand and by 1950 it had climbed to 3.6. By 1957 the birth rate peaked at 4.3. The rate then began to decline, but by 1964 it was still at 4.0. In real numbers that means from 1945 to 1964 over 78 million people were born. During the same period approximately 31 million died resulting in a population gain of 47 million.[23] Significantly for leaders, a large number of these people are still in the work force. As the largest generation in American history, Boomers found themselves in constant competition for recognition, attention, jobs, promotions, and everything else in society. But they didn't appear to start out that way.

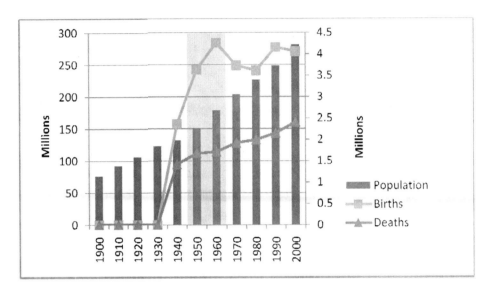

Figure 3.

Baby Boom Generation population, births and deaths [24]

America in the 1950s was an affluent and rapidly changing country. Veterans returning from war actively pursued education with the benefit of the GI Bill and were able to purchase new homes with the help of Veterans Administration home loan guarantees. Unemployment was very low, as low as 2.9% in 1953, and only reached the 5% and 6% range in the 1960s.[25]

The country began an unprecedented period of mobility with people moving for employment and traveling for pleasure. In 1930 the U.S. Census Bureau placed the population center of the country in western Indiana but reported that it had moved to western Illinois by 1970.[26] Under President Eisenhower the nation's interstate highway system improved, allowing easier travel around the country. Air travel was expensive but no longer out of the reach of a large share of the population. Easier travel tended to make the country seem a little smaller and more people began to experience things they had never seen before. As the nation expanded and people increasingly were able to own their own homes, new communities sprang up and suburban America was born. Entertainment became more readily available as television spread in popularity.

This was the most educated generation as well. In 1970, when the last of the Silent Generation was 25 years old 52% had achieved a high school diploma. By 1989, when the last of the Baby Boom Generation reached 25 years of age, 75% had earned a high school diploma, and 21% had completed at least one year of college.[27]

All was not rosy. The serious social issues that had been addressed by the Silent Generation came to the forefront. Women who had enjoyed industrial work, and wages, during World War II were now back to being housewives and mothers or were expected to revert to lower paying "women's" jobs. Having tasted a little independence, they yearned for more, a desire they transferred to their daughters in a big way. The Baby Boomers were the first generation to see women become a significant and permanent part of the workforce.

Even more serious were the race issues that emerged during the 1950s. Actually, race issues (primarily concerning black Americans) had been a concern since the founding of the nation but during the 1950s they became a primary source of unrest in much of the population. While many felt it was time to put an end to the systemic racial discrimination prevalent in the country, an end to discrimination and racial bias was not to occur quickly or painlessly. It would be an uphill battle.

It was into this turmoil that the Baby Boom Generation emerged. They grew up in more affluent circumstances than any previous generation and came to expect such comfort. Though not all parents subscribed to them, new theories of child rearing began to emerge, the most famous being Dr. Benjamin Spock's *Baby and Child Care,* which offered new ideas for a more gentle form of child rearing. The first Baby Boomers would reach their teen years in the late 1950s when much of the post-war glow had begun to fade and the more serious issues took center stage.

While the GI Generation tended to join organizations and think in terms of groups, the Baby Boom Generation was more self-absorbed, even narcissistic. Often called the "me generation" they were more likely to eschew the groups of their parents and grandparents in a search for individualism.

The fairly affluent and often somewhat care-free childhood and adolescence of the generation resulted in a much less disciplined adult who saw all the problems of the world, blamed those problems on their parents, and wanted to solve everything. This was probably the first generation, at least of the ones studied here, to have an almost zealous mistrust of their elders and most, if not all, organizations. With a very broad brush they called anyone not of their group "the establishment." A popular mantra of the generation's early years was "Don't trust anyone over 30." Interestingly, this quote is attributed to Jack Weinberg who was born in 1940, making him a member of the Silent Generation, not the Baby Boom.[28] This interesting dichotomy will show up several more times in our review of this generation.

The Baby Boomer's early years were filled with social unrest. They were the first generation to grow up with the television beaming images of trouble around the world directly into their living room. When Governor George Wallace stood at the door of the University of Alabama to prevent two black students from entering, young teens and adults saw the episode unfold on their televisions. When reports from Vietnam included graphic video of the horrors of war, those images were available for everyone to see. In spite of parent's attempts to give children a carefree life, the children saw serious problems in the world, and they wanted to act.

Racial tension was escalating as black Americans began to rebel against the treatment they had endured. In 1954, the Supreme Court decided in the case of Brown vs. the Board of Education of Topeka Kansas that segregation violated the 14th Amendment to the Constitution. The case, which actually combined five cases, revolved around the question of whether school districts should provide separate schools for black children or if they should be forced to integrate black children into the traditionally white-only schools.[29] Though the Baby Boom generation had nothing to do with this decision, they did see the results, and as they grew older took up the cause. In 1957, nine black students were to attend the Little Rock, Arkansas Central High School. Arkansas governor Orval Faubas attempted to block the students using the state's National Guard. President Eisenhower answered the challenge by federalizing the Guard and deploying regular Army troops, ensuring the students were allowed to attend.[30]

Probably the most compelling segregation related spectacle was the 1963 riot in Birmingham, Alabama. City police and firefighters attacked demonstrators with police dogs and fire hoses.[31] Images of these attacks were beamed around the world and the importance of that coverage cannot be overstated. This public event was instrumental in the passage of the Civil Rights Act of 1964.[32] The Baby Boom Generation quickly learned to rely on television, both as the best means to follow national and world events, and as a medium to spread their own interests and ideas. This use of visual media vastly increased throughout the life of this generation and the ones to follow.

Another cause taken up by the Baby Boom Generation (though certainly not started by them) was women's liberation. This "movement" actually traces its roots well into American history, but enjoyed its highest prominence during the Baby Boom Generation. A joint statement by six liberation groups in North Carolina sums up the basic beliefs of the movement. Specifically "They are working to eliminate the inequities of a system that oppresses groups such as women, blacks, and the poor. Some specific goals are equal education and job opportunities, equal pay for equal work, and the universal child care facilities without which such opportunities would be useless. But these goals were only part of the overall need for women to be able to freely make choices on matters which control their lives."[33] There were many different approaches to this feminist movement, some emphasizing women as individuals with the ability to do the same work and attain the same status as men while others were more interested in celebrating womanhood as an equal position with manhood. Again, key leaders in the women's movement, such as Gloria Steinem (born 1936) and Betty Friedan (born 1921) were from earlier generations, but gained the most traction when the Baby Boom generation began to come of age.

Women had been gaining an increasing presence in the working world for decades. In 1940 only 24% of the American work force was female. By 1950, that figure had risen to 28% and over the next three decades, the number would continue to rise; 32% in 1960, 37% in 1970, and 42% in 1980.[34]

Racial equality and women's liberation were two significant topics for the Baby Boom Generation but the Vietnam War would become the defining event of the generation's early years of adulthood.

Vietnam was a French colony prior to World War II. Japanese forces occupied the country during that war and ousted the French government. After the Japanese surrender, the country was first divided between China and England who were given responsibility to clear

Japanese soldiers from the northern and southern halves respectively. During the Potsdam conference in Europe, the allied leaders agreed to France's request for the return of their colonies in Southeast Asia. A Vietnamese insurgent leader Ho Chi Minh, who actually allied with the U.S. against the Japanese, now declared that Vietnam was a separate nation and should be free of French colonialism. The French weren't about to leave voluntarily though and military conflict ensued, eventually resulting in French defeat in 1954. During the waning days of the French conflict, the U.S. government decided to provide military support in a very limited way, but that limited support would continually increase until the U.S. military was involved in a full scale war. Decisions to escalate U.S. involvement were based on feelings of responsibility since the U.S. had set up the South Vietnamese government. Fear of the spread of communism also provided an impetus as Ho Chi Minh was receiving support from the communist governments in China and the Soviet Union.[35] In the democratic west, and primarily in the U.S., many leaders subscribed to the "Domino Theory" which postulated that if Vietnam fell to the communists, the rest of the region would follow like "falling dominos."[36]

Successive presidents; Eisenhower, Kennedy, Johnson, and Nixon increasingly failed to garner popular support for action in Vietnam. To complicate matters, the circumstances leading to American involvement in the conflict were complex and not well understood by the American public. The public believed, probably correctly, that the South Vietnamese government, for which American soldiers were fighting and dying, was corrupt.

Once again, the Baby Boom Generation would follow leaders, such as Jane Fonda (born 1937), and Tom Hayden (born 1939) from previous generations in protesting something they felt the previous generation was doing wrong. And, once again, television images would polarize the public and were a constant companion in American living rooms. Many in the anti-war movement burned draft cards and thousands went to Canada rather than serve in the military. The protests had the desired effect. A Gallup poll in 1965 indicated that 64% of Americans supported the war in Vietnam. By 1969 that number had dropped to 52% and by 1970, 55% felt the U.S. should bring all military forces home from Vietnam. [37]

The Baby Boom Generation was known as the generation of sex, drugs, and rock and roll. A common mantra was "turn on, tune in, drop out." Again though, note that phrase was coined by Timothy Leary, (born 1920) a counterculture icon who encouraged use of hallucinogenic drugs. Whether drug use was more common in the 1960s and 1970s than it is today is difficult to determine. There are numerous statistics on illicit drug use through the decades but their reliance on self-identification leads me to question their accuracy. I do believe though that there has never been another time when blatant, unapologetic use of illicit drugs was as much a part of American culture.

This brief review of the 1960s and early 1970s is what is commonly associated with the Baby Boom generation. I believe this is an unfair view though as most of the unrest of that era was led by activists who were older, in some cases considerably older, than the young people they led. Most of the activists of that period were from the Silent Generation though a few were even members of the GI Generation. This isn't to say that many Baby Boomers did not participate, and even enthusiastically support the causes of the day; they did. But they seldom led those efforts. It's true that for many members of that generation there is an almost rabid discontent with the status quo and a willingness to challenge authority, even to the point of breaking the law. Protesting was a common thing to do; almost a pastime. I was talking to a woman a few years ago, a member of the Boomer Generation, who lamented that she missed the protests and longed for a chance to hit the streets again. I asked her what she felt she needed to protest and she said it didn't matter. To her, it was not so much about what to protest but more about the exhilaration of actually doing it. I think that's a great example of what some in the Baby Boom generation actually learned from their early years -- being rebellious was an end unto itself.

That brings us back to Woodstock. This rock concert, or music festival as it was called, was put on by Michael Lang (born 1944) and was attended by approximately a half million people, mostly young Baby Boomers. Woodstock provides a sort of microcosm of the contradiction of the period when Baby Boomers were coming of age. Lang, who had experience with a similar but much smaller concert in Florida, wanted to put on a music festival that would be a three day celebration of music, art, and peace. In many ways he was very successful. The weekend was peaceful and really quite well organized considering the many difficulties the promoters encountered. Lang and his partners intended to make a profit, or at least not suffer a loss. Before the event began, $631,000 of tickets had been sold, but once the weekend started, the concert ended up being free. One of the reasons the concert ended up being free is that some groups, such as Abbie Hoffman's Hippies, (Abbie Hoffman was born in 1936) tore the fences down, allowing people to enter without using the gates. Adding to the problem were severe traffic jams caused by early arrivers, which prevented delivery of the ticket booths. What the attendees, and probably most of those analyzing the event then and later probably didn't realize was the negotiation that was necessary to sign the various bands that performed. In many cases the bands, usually under the orders of their managers, would not go on until they had been paid. After the event ended, the partners were left with large debt and a little less peace than the attendees had experienced. In fact, the corporation formed to promote the event, Woodstock Ventures, split apart when the members could not agree on who would be involved in future endeavors. Lang, the impetus behind the entire event, laments that he ended up losing what would have been millions from the subsequent, and inevitable, movie.[38]

Woodstock captures the essence of that era. It was at once a business venture, protest, art display, and peaceful concert. In the closing performance of Woodstock, Jimi Hendrix performed a version of the National Anthem that would be repeated often over the following years. It was loved and embraced by some and soundly hated by others. In Lang's own words;

"As he almost reverently started the national anthem, the bedraggled audience, worn out and muddy, moved closer together. Those of us who'd barely slept in three days were awakened, exhilarated by Jimi's song. One minute he was chording the well-worn melody, the next he was reenacting 'bombs bursting in air' with feedback and distortion. It was brilliant. A message of joy and love of country, while at the same time an understanding of all the conflict and turmoil that's torn America apart."[39]

It was a desire for change, but at its heart was a dislike of what a nation was doing, but without a dislike of the nation itself. After Woodstock, many of the half million attendees would go on to make the nation even greater.

So, what became of the Baby Boomers? By 1975, the Vietnam War had drawn to a close and the country was beginning to relax. It's important to understand that, though the Boomers are known as the rebellious, anti-everything generation, those were a minority, loud to be sure, but still a minority. More common were young people who didn't care that much about the political issues of the day or even found themselves on the polar opposite of the political spectrum.[40] The economy, which had been fairly strong to this point, began to falter and three periods of recession were to follow; the first in 1974 - 1975, the second in 1980, and the third in 1981 - 1982.[41] At the same time, the majority of Boomers were at the age when it became more important to have a job. Along with the Boomers' need for jobs and the declining economy came increased unemployment. From 1966 to 1969, unemployment had stayed below 4% but in the 1970s rose to 7% and by 1982 was near 10%.[42] But, even with the slower economy, Boomers became part of the "establishment" that many of them had so vehemently railed against only a few years before.

There is some belief that Boomers became rabid capitalists at the expense of parenthood; however, while Boomers certainly began to embrace capitalism, they didn't stop having children. In fact the birth rate began to increase in the mid to late 1980s and by 1988 had exceeded the birth rate for most of the 1970s.[43] What Boomers did do was continue with their jobs and often farm the kids out to daycare or relatives; the consequences of which we will examine in the next chapter.

As the large Boomer Generation entered the workforce they were, by necessity, competitive and looked for opportunities to advance. However, a change was occurring in the workforce that has resulted in a gradual decline in long-term tenure on the job. The decline has been steady for men, while women's long-term tenure actually increased for a short period, then declined. It's possible that the change in numbers of women in the workforce may be the result.[44] Boomer's desire to succeed did not stop as they aged. In fact, though entrepreneurship is currently more normally associated with younger generations; a 2009 study by the Ewing Marion Kaufman Foundation found that the largest group of entrepreneurs was in the 55 - 64 age groups.[45] Interestingly, boomers are not retiring as early as former generations. Many are now concerned that their retirement savings have been lost or at least severely degraded by the recession that began in 2008. A study by the American Society of Certified Public Accountants showed that 35% of those nearing retirement age are delaying that decision for at least 5 years.[46] With the rapid rise in unemployment that began in 2009, many of those Boomers, who still want to work, find themselves unemployed and therefore also a source of competition in the job market.

As the Boomers became part of the mainstream working world, they didn't lose their idealism. This generation often leans more to the left politically, and remains willing to take on causes such as concern for the environment and the still relevant women's and racial equality issues. In what may seem an odd turn of events, some of the staunchest anti-drug advocates are Boomer's. Of course there are no absolutes, and a recent article in the Washington Post points out that many older Boomers are becoming more likely to openly defy marijuana laws and partake in the occasional joint.[47]

In 2008, social commentator Jonathan Pontell proposed a theory that those born between 1954 and 1965 were not really part of the Baby Boom Generation. He claims they were too young to have participated, or even have been very concerned with the upheaval of the 1960s and 1970s and yet were not really part of the next generation, Generation X, either. He titles his new category Generation Jones. He bases much of his theory on the candidacy, and election, of Barack Obama, (born in 1961) as the indication that this new generation is now flexing its muscle.[48] Obama is one of the youngest presidents in U.S. history, (not <u>the</u> youngest; that would be Theodore Roosevelt) and was the first non-white male to be elected (his father is African and his mother is white). Indeed this does represent a change in American culture, but does it indicate that a separate generation has emerged from the last cohorts of the Boomers? Since Pontell's evidence supporting a new generational category centers on the election of Barack Obama, let's examine that election more closely.

This study is not about American politics; however, many times a nation's politics provides a window to its culture. The 2008 election was indeed a watershed event in the nation's history. The nation had the choice of selecting a black president, Barack Obama on the Democratic ticket, or a female vice-president, Sarah Palin on the Republican ticket. While not a landslide, Obama did carry a significant portion of the electorate and the election left no doubt that America was in the mood for change. The country was descending into what looked to be (and did become) a deep recession. Unemployment for the decade up to the election had averaged 5.1% and the economy was doing well.[49] Economists consider 5% to be full employment. By the November election unemployment had climbed to almost 7% and didn't appear to be turning around.[50]

An examination of who voted for Obama over his opponent, Republican Senator John McCain in the 2008 presidential election, reveals that voters aged 30 - 44 leaned slightly for Obama at 52% versus 47% for McCain, while voters aged 45 - 59 (the age of the proposed Generation Jones) were exactly split at 49% each. Earlier Boomer, GI, and Silent Generation voters chose Obama

47% and McCain 51%. The telling number is voters in the 18 to 29 year groups who voted for Obama 66% and McCain 32%.[51] A review of the 2004 presidential election age demographics indicates a similar situation where the youngest group tended to provide more votes for the Democrat over the Republican candidate.[52] We must use caution in making this sort of comparison though. Each election presents a different selection of candidates, and the issues of the day are different, and more importantly, are presented differently by the candidates.

Additionally, while a review of Congress' freshman class elected in 2008 reveals that 25 were born between 1954 and 1965, 19 are solidly in the Boomer years and 13 are in Generation X. Rounding out the class are 5 from the Silent Generation and 1 from the Millennial Generation. So, while the largest single group of newly elected officials in the 2009 congressional elections was born between 1954 and 1965, as a group they only represent 39% of the freshman class.

Does the 2009 election represent a break out of this age group from the Boomers? Using the election as a measure, as Pontell does, would suggest not. But are there other indicators? Pontell suggests that his Generation Jones "is poised to grab the mantle of leadership"[53] That seems natural, since this group is at the age that generally finds itself elevated to more responsible positions. A recent list of companies in Forbes magazine listed 20 which they felt were most promising. Of those, 13 are led by people born between 1954 and 1965.[54]

So why spend so much time on this? The question of whether there is a Generation Jones or not demonstrates an important part of any discussion of the generations. There will always be those who don't fit, or don't feel they fit in the category their birth year assigns them to. For instance, the early cohorts of the GI Generation have very different experiences than the latter ones. In the case of Boomers, the world of the first cohort in 1945 was very different than the world of the 1950 cohort, which was definitely different than the 1960 cohort. Those who were born on either end of a generational category may not strongly identify with the larger population of that category. As Pontell points out, the late Boomers were in their pre-teen years during the upheaval of the 1960s and 1970s. They were watching, but didn't necessarily understand what all the fuss was about. But what is significant is that they were at that 7 - 12 year age group which Erickson defined as the point where children begin to form moral values and recognize differences in people and cultures.

Unlike those before them, the Baby Boomers were a generation that experienced vast differences in parenting. While in previous generations the nuclear family tended to stay together, that began to change with Boomers as the divorce rate rose significantly. Along with the increased divorce rate came an increase in the number of divorced people who remarried, creating more complex family situations. Also increasing were the incidents of single women bearing children.[55] All together, these factors stood the traditional family unit on its head. But, there were and still are, different philosophies of child rearing, with some children growing up in an environment with little or no discipline and others living in more structured homes, reminiscent of earlier times. Also, though the television had joined the country in a new way, the interconnected society of today did not exist. While a child growing up in a rural area might see the images on the nightly news, the sources of those images were limited to the three major networks who all presented essentially the same information. For the most part, interpretation was left up to parents.

As mentioned before, the Boomers are a very large group and when they entered the workplace they became, by necessity, very competitive. The last cohorts of the generation came into this competitive environment late and felt a little disadvantaged. I find no long-term issue though and generally favorable employment figures would tend to indicate that even the late Boomers had little difficulty finding their way into society just as their older brothers and sisters had done.

In the midst of all this unrest and social turmoil, the Boomers were doing something which would make their children's world a completely different place. As I mentioned in the previous chapter, the computer age had dawned earlier, but it was Boomers who made personal computers in our homes and offices a reality. The big four who revolutionized computers and made them accessible to the everyday person, Steve Jobs, Steve Wozniak, Bill Gates, and Paul Allen, where all Boomers. Their development of Apple (Jobs and Wozniak) and Microsoft (Gates and Allen) changed the world in such a fundamental way that it's difficult to overstate. Probably owing to their competitive nature, Boomers were fairly eager to grasp the new technology and apply it to their lives. While some, especially from the earlier cohorts of the generation, were a little slow to adapt to this technological revolution, most did in a big way. It was the Boomers who first grasped the potential of the personal computer and made it part of their lives. But it could be argued that Boomers never really imagined what computers would become. That would be left to the next two generations.

# Chapter 4
# Generation X and the Millennials

Generation X

    Every generation complains that the previous generation just doesn't understand them. That lament is generally true, but with Generation X, it has risen to a whole new level. It seems impossible for Boomers to completely understand Xers, even though in many ways they are what Boomers thought they were going to be. They tend to not trust the establishment, seem less interested in material things, are often openly defiant of authority, and are generally more acceptant of drug use. In spite of this big generation gap, Xers seem to get along better with their Boomer parents than Boomers did with their parents.[1]

    The Boomer Generation was the largest, but they produced a much smaller generational group, known as Generation X, born between about 1965 and the late 1970s. Of the generational groupings, this is the shortest at only about 15 years compared to 20 years for the Boomer, Millennial, 18 for the Silent Generation, and 27 for the GI Generation. During the Xer Generation, a little over 37 million people were born (less than half the Baby Boom Generation) and slightly more than 19 million people died for a total population increase of almost 18 million.[2] The significance is notable when compared to the population increase of 47 million for Boomers and 36 million for Millennials. With many born into some very complex situations, with step-parents, single parents, multiple parental figures on the periphery of their lives (former step-parents), and half-siblings, this generation can be excused for feeling a little confused at times.

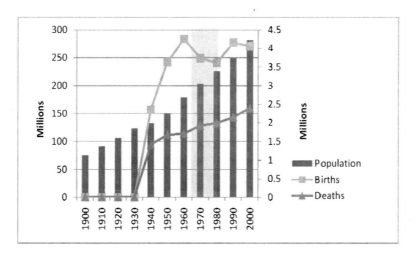

Figure 4.

Generation X population, births, and deaths [3]

Though there were few big world events in the Xers' early years, that isn't to say they haven't seen turmoil. The most significant event in their young lives was the end of communism in Russia with the resulting peaceful demise of the Soviet Union and the fall of the Berlin Wall. While these events, taken together or even separately, were seen by many Boomers as perhaps the most significant events in their lifetime, much of Generation X did not attach the same significance to them. It seems that every generation has to have a war, and for this generation it was the Gulf War known as Desert Storm. This successful effort to free the small country of Kuwait from the domination of its neighbor, Iraq, was over quickly with relatively few casualties meaning that Generation X did not experience a long bloody war as other generations had during their formative years. In stark contrast to the gore of Vietnam, delivered nightly into the living rooms of previous generations, the Gulf War seemed almost like a video game with footage of precision weapons and night vision scenes. Though there were some who protested the war as simply trading American lives for Middle Eastern oil, it was generally a popular expedition and many Boomers seemed to feel a need to soothe the wounds of the Vietnam era by enthusiastically supporting "the troops" even to the point of accepting a war they might not have completely agreed with.

What probably affected Generation X more than these world events was change and turmoil in the business world. Xers watched as the recession of 1982 - 1983 turned into the boom of the late 1980s; a boom that would last for the most part, through the next decade and into the new century. By the time the majority of Xers reached adulthood, the nation's economy was on a generally upward cycle. But, there were downturns such as the stock market decline in 1987 and the bust of the early internet, or dot com companies in the late 1990s. We'll revisit this important point in a few paragraphs.

Interestingly, many Xers did not see the 1980s and 1990s as a boom time. In his book *Managing Generation*

*X*, Bruce Tulgan, himself an Xer, laments this period as less than glorious.[4] What really was a generally rosy picture though, was to change in 2008 as the nation, and indeed the world, was plunged into a severe recession. The recession was a complete shock to most of a generation who had grown up during a period of prosperity and who had been taught leverage (borrowing) as a means of acquiring the better things in life. So, there was plenty happening, though not of the magnitude of a depression or world war. There was a significant event that did end up defining this generation, and the generation to follow - the computer revolution.

Xers did not create the technology boom, but they certainly did accelerate it and make it their own. From early childhood, this generation became the first to live at least part of their lives on-line. In their adult years, email became a normal part of life and there was already a significant body of information available on the World-Wide Web. If one was so inclined, friendships and romances could be carried on entirely in what would become known as cyber space without the participants physically meeting. Computer capability increased at an amazing rate. Moore's Law, named for Gordon Moore the co-founder of computer chip company Intel, states that the number of transistors on a computer chip will double every two years. Moore made this prediction in 1965 and hasn't yet been proven wrong.[5]

Generation X has experienced a social upheaval unlike that of previous generations. As already mentioned, many grew up in fractured homes. They watched their competitive Boomer parents conforming to a system Xers didn't understand. It often seemed the Boomer's single-minded quest for success while trying to manage their own complex lives left little room for their Xer offspring. Also, with more dual income families working hard to obtain their desired life style, Xers found themselves being cared for during a significant part of their early years by someone other than a primary parent. All this gave the generation a different and often mistrusting view of their world. Interestingly, Generation X often appears to be more anti-establishment than their Boomer parents ever thought about being.

To add insult to injury, when this generation was ready to enter the workforce, they found their Boomer parents still there and still very competitive. While previous generations were anxious to move up in the company, attaining ever higher levels of responsibility and more important sounding job titles, Xers, who in their early years had seen many of those companies fail, took a more pragmatic approach. They jumped from one job to another with more concern for development than advancement. Though this was foreign to their predecessors, the tactic has served them well, making them more broadly knowledgeable as well as more resilient to change.

On August 1st, 1981, at 12:01 AM a new phenomenon hit the airwaves when Music Television, known now as MTV, broadcast its first music video. Aptly title "Video Killed the Radio Star," this seemingly minor event signaled the beginning of a new era in entertainment. While cable television was not new, the 1980s saw an explosion of available channels and programming for those willing to pay. Unlike their Boomer parents, who somehow existed on only three networks, Xers had a vast selection of entertainment available. Combined with the rapidly growing capabilities of the internet, there were many alternatives to playing outside and face-to-face socializing in later years. One could meet a potential mate on-line, exchange history, interests, and even pictures (if willing to wait for the slow connection speeds of the day) without ever actually meeting. What had been a normal process to learn basic socialization skills was turned on its ear. Adding to this technological revolution was the video game. The first games (primitive by today's standards) appeared in arcades in about 1970 but by 1972 they had invaded the home market and young gamers could sit in front of a TV screen and shoot alien spaceships or bounce a pong "ball" around for hours.[6]

The result of this explosion of technology was to create an artificial world for young Xers who were growing up in a very different family situation than their Boomer parents. In their world, information flowed at a very rapid rate and there seemed to be no limit to the possibilities. While Boomers learned to cope with new technology and use it as a tool, it was an integral part of Xers lives. More importantly, Xers began to expect visual images. The written word, by itself, was no longer sufficient.

Xers grew up busy. There were countless activities, both social and athletic to occupy their time. They grew accustomed to always having something to do or somewhere to go as their Boomer parents tried to get keep them occupied.

Xers are the most educated generation yet. In 1990, 75% of the population 25 years and older had a high school education and 20% had at least a bachelors degree. In comparison, in 1970 the numbers were 52% and 11% and in 1980 it was 67% and 16% respectively.[7] They also came of age at a time when a vast, almost unending stream of information became available on the internet. There was no filter or peer review for most of this information though, and what was often "urban legend" or simply one person's opinion could quickly become a perceived fact. Xers, who were suspicious of everything except the internet, often went forward with misleading or even wrong information.

Generation X has a reputation for changing jobs and not sticking with anything as long as Boomers are used to. The Bureau of Labor Statistics completed a longitudinal survey in 2002 revealing that Boomers born between 1957 and 1964 held an average of 9.6 jobs from ages 18 to 36. The survey also revealed that there were fewer job changes and that jobs were held longer as the subjects aged. A similar survey has not yet been completed for Generation X; however, Farber's study (cited previously) seems to indicate an upward trend.[8] Rutgers University professor Joe Markert at Rutgers University recently found that 25% of hourly employees have been on the job for less than one year and 50% have been on the job less than 5 years. Certainly a different situation than Boomers are used to! He also found that most say they quit because of their boss. [9]

While trust on a large scale is impossible to accurately quantify, Generation X seems to be less trusting than other generations. As already discussed, many of them grew up with family situations that were less than favorable. When they reached working age, at least a portion of this generation was heavily invested (in an employment and financial sense) in the meteoric rise of technology companies. Beginning in about 2000, the bubble burst and what had become known as the dot com boom became a dot com bust with a large part of the pain being born by Xers.[10] There was a lot of money to be made for a short time in the tech industry and so naturally, there was also a lot of money to be lost. For those caught in the bust, this was a very serious and lasting wound. One person told me of going from a lucrative job in "Silicone Valley" to destitution almost overnight. Other scandals would serve to put the icing on the cake and cause a large portion of the generation to become, seemingly permanently, suspicious of the business world.

In 1980, Congress passed legislation that deregulated the savings and loan industry. Before the legislation savings and loan institutions were only allowed to invest in mortgages but with deregulation they were allowed to invest in anything they wanted. Adding to the volatility of the situation, federal insurance coverage was raised from $40,000 to $100,000. Unfortunately, some in the industry took this as a license to steal and property speculation took off. As the big savings and loan companies which had made huge, but unwise investments, began to implode liability fell to the government. By the mid 1980s the agency responsible for insuring savings and loans, the Federal Savings and Loan Insurance Corporation, had experienced so many claims that it was itself insolvent. As the entire situation began to unravel, it became clear to the public that large campaign contributions by savings and loan owners made politicians very hesitant to take quick, decisive action. [11]

Enron started out as a small gas company in Nebraska. Using a new idea to consolidate energy into a central bank, Enron grew and by 2000 it was the fourth largest company in America and enjoyed international reach. Unfortunately, most of Enron's business was a fraud. With some creative bookkeeping the company was able to present losses as profits and cover up a continual slide into bankruptcy. By the end of 2001 the curtain was pulled back and the full extent of the scandal became public. To make matters worse, investigation revealed that Enron executives had cashed out their stock immediately prior to the implosion, leaving the employee's pension plan high and dry.[12]

Douglas Coupland's novel *Generation X* hit the shelves in 1991. This was the first time the Generation X label had been used and it stuck. Since then many books and articles have appeared, some with studies comparing Xers with other generations; but, as with previous generations, future study will probably paint a different picture. What has been written so far tends to paint this generation in a fairly negative light. Even books and articles attempting to support Xers (usually written by Xers) often casts them in a less than flattering way; at least to members of other generations. Let's examine the charges levied against this generation.

1. Xers are skeptical and pessimistic. They do not care about titles and tend to eschew authority. There is a

lot of truth to this as one would expect from their history. Raised in fractured or downright broken families, they tend to have a natural distrust of what previous generations have considered "normal". Their parents, perhaps as a way to compensate for being away so much, tended to give them everything they wanted; or at least as much as they could afford. They grew up listening to parents (and step-parents and other caregivers) speak despairingly about bosses. When they entered the workplace, they noticed that everyone seemed to have a title and yet, the titles didn't seem to mean a whole lot.

2. Xers are the ultimate "me generation." This is easy to deduce from the way this generation tends to appear to be looking out for themselves. However, with the issues already discussed, it isn't difficult to see why. They often felt that they had to look out for themselves. Though their Boomer parents became loyal members of the company, Xers were more individualists. Add to that the fact that the Boomer generation is living and working longer and, from an Xer point of view, won't get out of the way.[13]

3. Xers are rude and don't understand etiquette in normal social situations. By Boomer standards, this is true. By Xer standards though, Boomers are too stuck in old ways. A fairly strict, if unwritten set of behavioral rules have developed for social media on-line and these rules sometimes differ greatly from rules familiar to previous generations. Xers do seem to have great difficulty mastering communication with members of the previous generations. Interestingly, there seems to be a general

feeling among Xers that the subsequent generation, the Millennials, suffers from the same problem.

4. Xers haven't had any adversity in their lives. For the most part, when compared to previous generations, this is true. I must caution though that such a statement doesn't take into account the great differences in where and how they were raised. Much of what has been written by Xers indicates a feeling that they lived through the terrible economic times of the 1980s and 1990s. Since those were demonstrably some of the best economic times since probably the mid-1920s, this feeling is difficult for their elders to understand. This attitude can be attributed to three factors. First, many Xers were just entering the workforce during this time and many of them were quickly absorbed by the burgeoning high tech industry. Many also invested heavily in what was called the dot com boom. When that boom went bust in the late 1990s, many lost significantly.[14] This was a new industry and many of the tech companies of the 1980s did not survive. Second, as discussed earlier, Xers were raised in much less secure circumstances than their parents had been and the resulting independence tended to cause a problem in the workplace where Boomer, and even Silent Generation supervisors, didn't understand them. Finally, in the internet era of today, anyone can write anything and garner a fairly large audience. While people tend to be more vocal about things that displease them, people also seem more likely to agree with those who they feel represent that discontent. People who are happy don't write about it nearly as much.

When I ask people about conflicts in the workplace, one of the most common complaints is that Xers don't want to acknowledge their Boomer bosses and co-worker's experience. At the same time, Xers complain that Boomers don't want to help Xers succeed. Obviously, there is a communication problem. One Boomer complained about a committee of Xers formed to develop services for Boomer retirees. When she tried to help with suggestions, the Xer team told her she didn't understand what the team needed. Another Xer complained that Boomers don't want to teach and mentor younger workers.

## The Millennials

If Xers ushered in the computer age, Millennials <u>are</u> the computer age. They are more comfortable with technology than any generation before them. This is a young generation though and as we discuss younger generations, the definition becomes more uncertain as there is still little data and few complete studies available.

Generally, Millennials (also called Generation Y) are considered to be those born between 1980 and 2000, but only time will tell if that's accurate. In the Millennial Generation, there were a little over 81 million births and slightly less than 46 million deaths resulting in a population increase of a just under 36 million. Millennials are now the largest generational group![15] The increased death rate is significant as it represents the rapidly accelerating demise of the GI Generation.

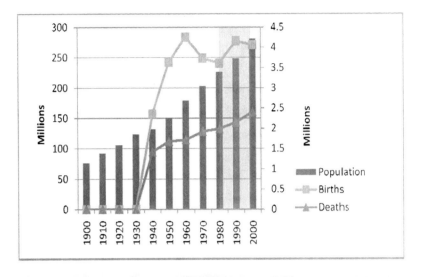

Figure 5.

Millennial Generation population, births, and deaths [16]

This generation may seem to be homogenous, but as more of its members enter the workforce they will certainly demonstrate a wide range of behaviors. Because of the size of the generation and an unusually broad variation in parental generations, that variety may be more than was seen in any other generation. The age of birth mothers has increased markedly since 1980. In 1980 73% of mothers were between the ages of 18 and 29 while 19% were between 30 and 44. By 2000, those numbers had changed to 35% and 62% respectively. Millennials are actually the offspring of three previous generations!

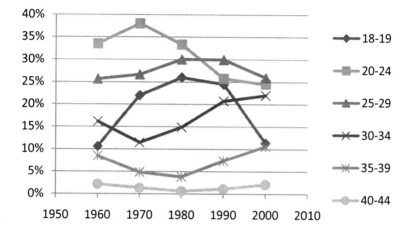

Figure 6.

Age of Birth Mothers[17]

The Millennial Generation came of age in the late 1990s, a time of economic prosperity and low unemployment and is just now beginning to create a definition for itself. The earliest cohorts of the generation had just graduated from high school when the short recession of 2001 occurred, but most were not greatly affected by it. The terrorist attacks of September 11, 2001 occurred when about half of this generation was reaching adulthood. That event certainly left a lasting impression, but the subsequent military actions in Iraq and Afghanistan did not result in the nationwide protest and violence that accompanied the Vietnam War in the 1960s and 1970s. What will probably be a bigger event to Millennials is the severe recession that started in 2008.

The Millennial Generation grew up very differently than their parents. They were much closer to their parents and lived through a period in which the whole world seemed concerned with children's self esteem. Even though their parents were from three previous generations, many of those parents seem to be trying to overcompensate for previous absentee parenting and were often an ever-present part of their children's growing-up years. No scrapped knee or bruised ego went untreated. Many Millennials learned that just showing up, not necessarily on time, was reason for praise and reward and that not only was failure not an option, it really wasn't even a serious consideration. They lived their youth in a world that seemed to be set up just for them.

Their world moves fast. Everything seems to happen at light speed including communication. There is no time for long, drawn out explanations. At the same time, communication is constant. Whether by email, cell phone, or text messaging, it seems Millennials are always communicating with someone. They far exceeded the Xers as denizens of the internet society with a significant portion of their social experience occurring on-line. They are very comfortable, more so than any group previously, with technology in any form. They quickly adapt to changes in technology that leave previous generations with a headache. They also use technology tools in innovative ways such as on-line social networking sites and the ubiquitous Twitter. Millennials exist on-line and they want others to know they're there.

While Generation X found that the internet provided a vast new source of information, Millennials have embraced the web as the only real reliable source. They will judge a potential employer by their website. They are as comfortable buying on-line as actually going into a store. If they want information, they turn to the search engines. An On-Line Community Library Center newsletter cites studies showing just how dependent this generation is on the internet, quoting one Millennial as saying, "Google is my first place to find something quickly." "I wouldn't really trust my librarian. I trust Google." "[Google] is user friendly ... [the] library catalog is not." Surprisingly, they also found that Millennials will not hesitate to ask parents, who apparently are more than willing to shortcut the research process with quick answers.[18] Unfortunately, this generation may not approach the information gleaned from Google or other such sources with a critical eye. Likewise, they will often default to a technological activity as opposed to a more traditional one. This was clearly demonstrated to me when I watched by grandchildren bowling...on the TV using the Wii game system. They expended quite a bit of energy with the game, but in the comfort of the living room. As my wife and I watched we commented that it seemed kind of strange to spend so much money on a system that simulates bowling instead of actually going bowling. The children (and their Xer parents) were dumbfounded and the only answer or justification we could illicit from them was that the Wii version was more "cool."

While this total immersion in technology is a critical part of their lives, it has been a little over stated as a part of their developmental years. While computers are a vital part of the Millennial's story now, what was more important to their earlier developmental years were the ever more sophisticated video and computer games which resulted in what is a fundamentally different way of processing information. Because their sources of entertainment moved at higher speeds, Millennial children's brains developed the ability to process information at a much faster rate. Also, Millennials were young at the same time the home computer was young and the two grew up together resulting in a sort of synergism that no other generation had experienced. Marc Prensky summed it up well saying,

"But the most useful designation I have found for them is **Digital Natives**. Our students today are all "native speakers" of the digital language of computers, video games and the Internet.

"So what does that make the rest of us? Those of us who were not born into the digital world but have, at some later point in our lives, become fascinated by and adopted many or most aspects of the new technology are, and always will be compared to them, **Digital Immigrants**."

Digital immigrants may have learned the language and adopted the culture, but like most other immigrants, they will always have an "accent" while digital natives do not have that previous culture ingrained in them and are therefore without an "accent."[19]

It's important to remember that while Millennials and home computers did grow up together, few Millennial children grew up with the high tech they are so adept at using today. Other than the early home computers already mentioned, most Millennials didn't see high levels of technical capability that was easily available until their late teen and young adult years. The first text message was sent in 1992, but the technology did not become easily accessible until several years later.[20] The personal computer was just becoming useful in the home as more than a sophisticated toy in the mid 1990s. America On-Line, the first popular source of email to the home computer user did not debut until 1985, but real access to such capability didn't really exist on a large scale for another 10 years.[21] Overall though, this generation seems to have a vastly improved ability to adapt to and assimilate new technology.

The ability to multi-task is also closely associated with Millennials as they text message while listening or participating in a conversation. Unfortunately, this tendency has progressed to text messaging while driving. An American Psychological Association study casts doubt on this capability. The study demonstrated that the human brain doesn't really multi-task but rather, rapidly switches between tasks. This makes it seem tasks are being done simultaneously, but they aren't. The time required to switch, is only fractions of a second, but it adds up.[22] While the brain may not really multitask, Millennials have demonstrated an ability to think in a more expansive, parallel and less linear way, rapidly processing information from multiple sources.

All this makes the Millennial Generation seem to be somewhat alien to their seniors. As noted previously, each generation tends to experience a sort of disconnect with the generation before them. Often called the generation gap, this chasm tends to narrow over time as the new generation matures and the older generation learns how to better relate. Such a generation gap exists with Millennials as well, but it is more like the Grand Canyon because in this case, the younger generation tends to be not only different in their world view, but different in the fundamental way they acquire, process, and use information.

When they started hitting the workplace Millennials, who had learned to obtain information, socialize, and even live their lives on the internet ran headfirst into a world that wasn't quite ready for them. On the one hand, Millennials grew up in a world that taught them they could always win, or at least be rewarded for participating, then joined a society that didn't work that way. On the other hand, Xers and Boomers have trouble understanding the fundamental difference in the way Millennials think. Their ability to process information at high speed and their reliance on technological means is not just a habit they picked up but the result of the way their brains grew and developed. In other words, it wasn't to be changed easily or at all at the most fundamental level. For the first time, the older generations would have to learn to adapt to the younger generation. That's made more difficult by the fact that Millennials have generally not mastered the skills of human social interaction and often find they are ill-prepared for a "real world" that's not interested in catering to their needs and where there are no rewards for just showing up.

# Chapter 5
# Gender Issues and Immigrants in the Workplace

## Gender Issues

There are two other topics that, while certainly an issue in earlier years, have become more significant with later generations: women in the workplace and immigration. Though perhaps not strictly generational issues, these two concerns factor into the overall discussion of differences between the generational groups. It's important for leaders to understand how these two issues are impacting the attitude of the newest generations more than previous ones.

As previously discussed women were not a large component of the workforce prior to World War II. Those women who did work were usually employed in what were at that time traditionally female roles such as teachers, secretaries, and nurses. After World War II, men who had been in the military returned to the workforce, displacing the women who had been doing the men's jobs while they were away. Most of these women dutifully returned to their home lives, birthing and raising the Baby Boom generation, but the seed had been planted and the number of women in the workplace would grow steadily. (See Table 1) As the Boomer generation emerged, what had

71

been a quiet acceptance (if not an embrace) of gender roles became a seething resentment of "male domination." Boomer women had no intention of being June Cleaver, and in their young adult years launched a full scale assault on the status quo.[*]

| Census Year | Percentage of Female Population Employed |
|---|---|
| 1940 | 25.0 |
| 1950 | 29.0 |
| 1960 | 34.5 |
| 1970 | 39.4 |
| 1980 | 49.9 |
| 1990 | 56.8 |
| 2000 | 66.0 |

Table 1[1]

There has been considerable discussion for many years about gender equality in the workplace. There are

---

[*] June Cleaver was the family's mother in the 1957 - 1963 television series "Leave it to Beaver." At the time, the character of June Cleaver was considered the epitome of an American wife and mother who cooked, cleaned, took care of children; but didn't "work."

numerous studies on this issue that all seem to indicate that women, as a rule, earn less than men. A study published in the Journal of Economic Issues concludes that women's pay differential for supervisory positions is a negative 9%. The study also concluded that marital status and whether a person is shy or outgoing has significant effect on supervisory opportunities and wages.[2] A 2008 study by the U.S. Bureau of Labor Statistics paints a very similar picture but shows that compensation rates for women have grown dramatically since 1979.

In fact, among women with a college degree the rate of growth is almost double that of men with a college degree. The study also showed that married women earn more than unmarried women but women with children earned less than women without children. Interestingly, while married men also earned more than their unmarried counterparts, the statistics for men with children were the opposite of those for women.[3]

Why do women earn less than men? It's a very contentious issue and the volumes written on the subject would probably circle the Earth, but it is very difficult to find hard data. There are several reasons that are normally citied to explain the pay disparity.

1. Historically, women did not earn as much as men because any income they made was considered supplemental to the male, head-of-household. Laws to prevent such inequity have only been partially successful. Silent Generation and even Baby Boom leaders may still see that difference as normal and acceptable. Most companies do not allow discussion of wages between workers and so specific disparities that show up in

surveys may not actually be known among the workers themselves. However, in spite of those rules, employees talk, which may serve to help reduce the disparity in the coming years.

2. Various studies show that men work more hours than women. Other studies show that many women work more hours than men. It is true though that, in general, those who work fewer hours are paid less, which accounts for some, but not all the disparity. As more men are sharing, or completely assuming primary child-care responsibilities in younger families, this dynamic may change.

3. Women have not been in the workforce as long as men and therefore have not attained the positions that would result in higher wages. This was probably true 20 or even 10 years ago; however, the studies cited above indicate that the pay disparity is evident in direct comparison; job-to-job. Also, women are more likely to be in lower paying careers and have yet to become comfortably ensconced in C-level offices of the largest corporations. Catalyst Research showed that, among Fortune 500 companies in 2009, only 15.7% of corporate officers, 15.2% of board seats, and 6.7% of top executive earners were women. But, 51.4% of managerial and professional positions were held by women.[4] That isn't to say that women aren't an important part of American business leadership. In fact, over 10 million firms are owned by women and generate $1.9 trillion in revenue. One in five of those businesses generate revenue over $1 million.[5]

The pay disparity issue became a growing problem when large numbers of Boomer women entered the workplace. They made some progress but obviously there is still a problem. Although Boomers often rebelled, they were also in a more competitive situation to keep their jobs. As Xers entered the workplace, their more open rebelliousness and greater willingness to move from job to job made pay inequality or even the perception of it a bigger issue for corporate leaders. How Millennials will deal with this issue remains to be seen, but leaders should be prepared to meet it head on. It is clear though that both Xer and Millennial workers will expect women to have equal access to all opportunities and to receive equal compensation.

The general attitude about women in the workplace has changed drastically. A study by the Families and Work institute showed that, in 1977, 74% of men and 52% of women surveyed felt that men should earn the money and women should stay home and raise the children. In 2002 those numbers had changed to 42% and 37% respectively.[6] In 1977, when asked if a women could have just as good a relationship with children when she worked outside the home, as when she didn't, 49% of men and 70% if women answered yes. By 2002, those numbers had changed to 64% of men and 78% of women.[7] Even more significantly, even though the study found no difference between older men and those under 30 (late cohort Xers), 73% more men under 30 felt that a mother who worked outside the home could have just as good a relationship with her children as one who didn't, compared to 62% for men over 30. Among women surveyed, there was no difference between younger and older women in their answers to that question.[8]

## Immigration

The second issue that carries greater significance to Xers and Millennials is the influx of new workers who are first or even second generation Americans. Leaders must understand that workers from other cultures, while American now, have different experiences and were taught by parents with different cultural backgrounds. From 1951 to 1971 the rate of immigration doubled from 1.7 to 3.4 per thousand and has continued to rise. By 1991 the rate had increased more than 4-fold to 7.3 per thousand. Immigration has since decreased but not to the level of the 1970s.[9] The two largest immigrant groups are from Asia and Central and South America.[10] From a cultural point of view; however, these are very inaccurate groupings. The Asian group can include anyone from a wide array of Asian countries from China to India, none of whom would consider themselves like the others. Likewise, the Hispanic label can include those from Mexico, South American countries, Puerto Rico, or even Caribbean countries. Unfortunately, these are the labels used in collecting data so we're stuck with them.

In a 2008 report, the U.S. Department of Labor identified 18% of the workforce as either Asian or Hispanic.[11] Both groups will continue to grow in the coming years. Though many in the workplace will be in the younger generations, in some ways they will exhibit the tendencies of older generations. Both Asian and Latin American countries have suffered severe financial hardships. Most of Asia enjoyed a rapid rise in prosperity after World War II, but that economic boom time came to a screeching halt in the 1990s. Japan has suffered a steep economic down-turn that started in the early 1990s and is only now beginning to abate.[12] Many other Asian nations saw economic progress beginning in the 1970s that began to lift them from poverty to affluence over the next 2 decades. A severe recession in 1997 and 1998 affected most of the Pacific Rim and while the Asian nations have recovered, the earlier boom times have not completely returned.[13] India has experienced over 60 years of a troubled economy and is only now beginning to emerge as a viable economic force.[14]

The immigrant Asian population enjoys a high level of educational achievement. In fact, the Department of Labor reports that the Asian population has a higher number of bachelor degrees than any other group in the study.[15] This is even more significant when one considers that many of their home countries had extremely poor rates of education until the 1970s when greater emphasis was placed on educational achievement. This vast improvement in education has been a catalyst for their economic growth and is something Asian immigrants have brought to this country.[16] Another factor that separates Asian immigrants from Xers and Millennials is war. With the exception of the attack on Pearl Harbor, Americans have not seen real armed conflict on American soil since the Civil War. Some Asian immigrants; however, have lived through war in their backyard. They have come here to experience peace and prosperity and they will work hard to take advantage of the opportunity they see. As of 2007, over 40% of Asian workers were in management, professional, or related positions.[17, 18]

Most Hispanic immigrants come from nations that have not enjoyed significant economic progress and have not placed emphasis on education. They too come to America to take advantage of the opportunity for prosperity, but they are educationally less prepared. The Department of Labor reports that only two thirds of the Hispanic population has completed high school, though education rates are slowly improving.[19] Like the Asian population, the younger Hispanic population either has experienced much less affluent times or has been told of such circumstances by parents or close relatives. It is important to note that the immigrant, especially Hispanic, population is booming. As of 2008 in New Jersey, California, Arizona, and Texas, Caucasians are no longer the majority.[20]

# Chapter 6
# But That Isn't Me!
# Those Who Don't Fit

There is a danger in grouping humans into categories. No matter how well-defined those categories are, someone will be left out or placed where they don't feel they belong. When dealing with groups as large as the generations, this isn't just a danger, it's an unavoidable fact. Many, when reading the definition of the generation they fall into by birth, agree the description might be correct but don't feel it describes them personally. There are primarily two reasons: the culture in which they were raised, and the part of the generation in which they fall chronologically.

Most common are the differences resulting from upbringing and culture. As I mentioned when discussing immigrants, there are considerable cultural differences from one part of the country to another. Someone raised in a small mid-western town will have different experiences than someone who grew up in a large metropolitan area. In fact, someone raised in New York City will have very different experiences than someone raised in Los Angeles. For late Boomers and early Xers, these differences have been compounded by technology as those in more rural areas were not as exposed to the world of the internet as quickly as those in more urban areas.

That gap is closing rapidly as technology works its way into every corner of the nation.[1]

I'll use myself as an example. I was raised in a fairly strict and conservative home. Traveling around the country in a microbus trying to "find ourselves" was just not something my sisters or I would have done. We stayed in school, applied ourselves, (them more than I) and wouldn't have known where to get drugs if we'd wanted to. I remember a protest in the city were we lived then that quickly boiled over into a full-fledged riot. We didn't get involved, nor did any of my friends. The counterculture pretty much passed us by!

This disparity in experience was especially evident in the 1960s and 1970s. There's a saying that if you can remember the '60s, you weren't there.[2] It's a little unclear where "there" was but the point is, there were many different experiences during that time. A young man who attended Woodstock mentioned that he and his friends were surprised to see so many "hippies" and "freaks" like them. He didn't think there were that many! [3] Though there is certainly a common thread running through the Boomer Generation, it is unfair, and unwise to paint them all with the brush of the protest period.

Though not as clearly defined, Generation X also has many who don't fit the normal definition. Much of Generation X is defined by how they were raised and here again, where they were raised most likely had a big effect. While the generation is normally associated with a demise of the nuclear family, that wasn't the case everywhere. There were certainly many Xers who grew up in what previous generations would consider a fairly normal family. But, at least through my Boomer eyes, Xers are a more consistent group than Boomers.

Millennials are a different matter all together. Marc Prensky believes that video games have a lot to do with the fundamental differences in Millennial brain structure.[4] Though as we saw in Chapter 4, Millennials come from very diverse parentage, video games seem to have been a common, overwhelming presence in Millennial's lives and were instrumental in teaching them to think in that fundamentally different way. With that saturation of the generation, it's conceivable they will be the most inclusive group yet. An additional factor is, as was previously mentioned, Millennial's parents were much more involved in their earlier lives.

The other problem with our generational groupings is that the start and end points are not clearly defined. The boundaries normally set for each generation tend to follow events rather than strict chronological periods. The groups are large enough that they include people who had very different views of those events. For instance, the early Silent Generation saw the depression at a young age, and though they were too young to fight, World War II. Even the late Silent Generation, which was too young to experience the depression, certainly learned about it in great detail as it was fresh in the minds of parents and older siblings. As I mentioned before, the fall of the Berlin Wall and the end of communism in the former Soviet Union was probably one of the biggest events in the lives of Boomers, their parents, and even some Xers, but younger Xers and Millennials did not have the life experience to appreciate the significance of those events.

In their work on generations in the workplace, Lancaster and Stillman have identified these people who find themselves in the first or last cohorts of a generation as "cuspers" because they exist on the cusp between one generation and the next. They mention that, sometimes these people can have success in bringing the generations together because they can cross experiences.[5] The idea of "cuspers" may be too narrow a definition. There are some in a generation's central cohorts that, because of how they were raised, where they were raised, or other personal experiences, tend to feel a closer connection to another generation. They aren't "cuspers" but they have the same feelings of not belonging. But as Lancaster and Stillman point out, people who find themselves balancing between generations or just not fitting in are in a unique place to be a bridge between the groups they straddle.

So why is it important to study the generations if there are so many exceptions and so many different people? Simply because it provides a starting point for a leader to begin to understand his or her people. Though there are exceptions, the various generations do have much in common and that understanding will help the leader gain a little better insight into what leadership methods will work better with each person. It isn't an inflexible formula and understanding generations is just the first step to better leadership.

Combining this knowledge of the generations, the leader can apply leadership principles in a more specific and targeted way that can defuse inter-generational tensions by taking advantage of the unique attributes of each one.

# PART II

# Chapter 7
# Leading the Generations

The company is owned by a member of the Silent Generation. Most of the company's senior leadership positions are held by Baby Boomers, though some Xers have worked their way to that level and actually supervise older Boomers. Middle management is a combination of Boomers and Xers supervising Millennials, many of whom have been recently hired. The company's two best clients are an older, well-established firm that looks very much like them, and an internet enterprise owned by an Xer who has a small staff whose average age is about 26.

This example illustrates a complex situation that is not uncommon! Probably more than at any time in history a greater number of multiple, and very different, generations occupy the same workplace and interact with each other. Add to that a fundamental shift in the dependence on technology for even the most basic tasks. The result can be conflict and disaster. But, when properly managed, these same ingredients can bring about a terrific opportunity for success! The leader's task is to bring it all together, avoid conflict when possible, and manage it when it can't be avoided. And yes, there will be times when it can't be avoided.

What must a leader do to be successful in this dynamic environment? It takes a combination of knowledge and skill: the knowledge of people and what motivates them and the skill to bring out the best in people no matter their age.

Leaders need knowledge about the general experiences of the generations. One of the interesting things that became apparent in my research is that most authors who write on this subject approach it from the perspective of their own generation and their own experiences. It seems when they refer to other generations, it's often in a way that, if not actually negative, at least is not with glowing praise. Successful leaders cannot allow themselves to look on other generations as better or worse; only potentially different.

In my research, I have found a phenomenon that I call generational adoption. Quite simply, this is when one generation, usually older, adopts something from another generation, usually younger. This is most evident in technology. Boomers, who didn't grow up with technology as later generations would, have adapted quite well and many now find a need for computers and cell phones just like their younger offspring. Most Boomers can remember their first color TV and how that was the height of progress at the time. Once a family had a color TV (usually only one per household) they were set! In contrast to their earlier years, many Boomers are quick to head to the store for the latest (or largest) model newly available this year. This concept of generational adoption is important for leaders to consider as it can further confuse the issue, making it difficult to sort out generational differences. What's important is that even if a worker appears to have adopted something from another generation, that fact does not change their life experiences, the overall way they view the world, or what motivates them at a basic level.

The differences in the generations lead to another critical area of knowledge necessary for good leadership, especially in a multi-generational situation. This will require a little "Leadership 101" study because some of the basic principles of human behavior haven't changed that much. People still have needs and respond to different motivators. As is true in any leadership situation, getting to know who subordinates are is critical to success. That's just more difficult when a multitude of generations occupy the same space.

Once acquired, it takes a certain amount of skill for leaders to effectively use this knowledge. Again basic leadership skill will probably need to be modified to fit the different groups. Much basic leadership and management theory is the result of the study of organizations in the 1960s and 1970s. These organizations were usually led by members of the GI or Silent Generation with Boomers working their way through the ranks. That dynamic has changed and two more very different generations have joined the workforce, adding new issues for a leader to deal with.[1] However, the basic theories they produced are still valid today and provide a basis for an adaptive leadership style which adjusts to the dynamic workplace of today.

The leaders challenge is three-fold. First, recruit the right people, second retain the right people, and third, provide an environment that allows them to grow and be as productive as possible. These steps have become more difficult than they used to be, requiring different techniques for different people. But, there are still some basic principles that transcend the generations.

Before we proceed, I want to briefly discuss the one absolute above all else. Leaders must have a set of values and must know what they are. Those values cannot be situational! A mistake made by too many leaders is an attempt to adapt their values to the people they are leading. That never works! One fact that's common to all generations is the need to know the genuine person. Most people have an innate ability to sniff out anything less and even those who don't agree with a particular set of standards are more likely to respect and follow a leader who stands by those standards than one who changes with the wind, making it difficult to know what he or she is thinking.

So, as we move ahead and apply some leadership principles to the generational conundrum, remember that the most important thing for a leader to do is know their people. This is so important you'll see it as a continual thread throughout the following chapters.

# Chapter 8
# What You Want is Not What I Need

One of the big conflicts between generations is a difference in what the various groups need. For people who lived through the depression, needs are more along the lines of a good job that pays a sufficient wage to support a family in relative comfort. As Boomers reached middle age, things that earlier generations might have considered extras tend to become needs. Xers have shown that they don't necessarily have the same need for material things but they do feel a strong need for self-fulfillment.

Is it important to know what people really need? Yes! Unfortunately, determining what they need is usually not a simple matter. In 1943, behaviorist Abraham Maslow published his famous Hierarchy of Needs. Maslow's hierarchy presented an ascending series of human needs, each of which was required to be met before the next level could be achieved. Once a particular need is met, the person can move to the next level; however, it's important to note that these needs do not go away just because they've been met. Lower level needs must continue to be met even while a person is striving to satisfy higher level needs. As an example, a pilot who ejects from a military aircraft very quickly goes from satisfying high level needs to basic survival needs. For a time anyway, those higher level needs are not very important.

Maslow said that everyone has basic physiological needs like warmth, shelter, and food. Once these needs are met, a person moves on to safety needs, specifically freedom from threat of physical or emotional harm.

After meeting their safety needs, a person moves on to what Maslow called higher level needs. The first of these, social needs, includes a feeling of belonging and love. When a person feels a sense of belonging, they can move to the next level, self esteem or a feeling that he or she has some importance to the world. The person wants to feel they've accomplished something and enjoy the attention and recognition that goes with that.

The highest level on Maslow's hierarchy is self-actualization -- the quest to reach his or her maximum potential. Maslow believed this need was never completely satisfied as the journey to self-actualization would always present new opportunities. He also believed that only a limited number of people ever reach this level.[1]

Maslow expanded his theory in 1954, publishing a manuscript titled "Eupsychian Management" in which he argued that a person's motivations change as they move up on the hierarchy of needs. Someone at the lower level, concerned with physiological or safety needs might be motivated by a higher paying job, while someone at a higher level will be more likely motivated by creative opportunities or assuming independence. He concluded that effective managers must have different policies for different people in different situations.[2]

Though Maslow's work is sometimes dismissed as unsophisticated by today's standards, his Hierarchy provides the basics for dealing with different generations.

Let's look at the basic needs. Regardless of age or generational grouping, everybody has a basic physiological need for food, clothing, and shelter. The problem is defining that need. By the 1950's, with the depression a memory, the need for food and shelter was generally met with steady jobs. Small, basic houses were built at a very rapid rate resulting in an explosion of suburban living.

Along came the Boomers who wanted more. Now shelter might mean a larger house and survival needs included packaged foods. Where their parents may have washed clothes by hand, a washing machine was now a necessity. Families no longer sat beside the radio to listen to Fibber McGee and Molly. Now television was the thing to have and became a need. The perceived survival needs of the Xer and Millennial Generations are much different than their parent's or grandparent's. As an example, a federal program provides cellular phones and service to people who qualify for some federal low income programs.[3]

So, what's the real need? Of course, a cave to live in, a fire for warmth and cooking, animal skins to wear and food available on the hoof would meet most actual human survival needs, but we have become programmed for more and, unless something really catastrophic happens, those elevated expectations become needs. So, is it the leader's responsibility to meet those needs? Yes and No. What the leader should be exploring is not just need, but perceived need. That's what will make a person feel satisfied and if the leader is not meeting a person's perceived needs, that person may move on.

For the Silent Generation, that perceived need is probably a secure job and wages sufficient to meet the necessities in life. Of course they have most likely adopted some of the perceived needs of later generations and so might feel a need for a larger house. Also, many of the older generations feel they have paid their dues and are owed a certain amount as well.

A Boomer also feels a need for these same things, though many have developed a perceived need for more material things. Many Boomer families became very accustomed to two incomes with the large influx of women in the workplace and with that income the ability to acquire those things they wanted. As previously noted, there are several reasons for the increase in the numbers of working women; but a definite influence was also the souring economy of the 1970s. By the mid 1980s the economy was on track to recovery, but the number of two income families did not significantly decrease. Keeping up and improving their lifestyle became more of a need than a want and their jobs provided the means to meet those perceived needs.

The younger generations, Xers and Millennials, have a different view of survival needs. Yes, they still need food and shelter, but they may perceive that need differently. As discussed in Part I, these generations are much more comfortable changing jobs and, while they have those basic needs, they may feel that they can be fulfilled in other ways, such as moving back with parents or temporarily living with friends. Xer's perceived needs are generally less materialistic and more personal. Xers are more likely to insist on family time rather than overtime, a desire probably stemming from a lack of family cohesiveness in their younger years.

Millennials have grown up in a world that seemed to give them everything they wanted, including plenty of parental attention. For many, their basic needs have always been met, driving them to more material types of perceived needs. They may feel a cell phone is a basic survival need and few don't have a computer. It's much too early to tell what affect the economic difficulties and high unemployment rate of the recession that began in 2008 will have on the Millennial Generation but I suspect, for at least some, it will modify perceived needs. The sudden rise in the unemployment rate may return them to a concern for more basic survival needs.

Up to now, I've only referenced basic survival needs. Maslow's hierarchy discusses other types of needs. In his hierarchy he places safety after survival saying that once a person is assured of survival, safety becomes the next concern. There was a time when workplace safety was not a genuine concern but in the last few decades, occupational safety has become a critical responsibility of all leaders. Therefore, physical safety is not really a generational issue. However, all generations want to also feel secure from personal assault, not just physical, but also mental. Though many would like to think this isn't an issue, it is. While members of the GI, Silent, and Boomer Generations were less likely to be concerned with what the lawyers might call mental anguish, the world has changed and now leaders must be careful of offending workers, even if it is unintentional. The cascade of diversity and sensitivity training that many organizations make mandatory are often in response to claims of a personal affront from an individual or group. Such issues create a concern for the safety need just as lack of machine guards might.

After survival and security, Maslow's Hierarchy moves to higher level needs. At these levels, a perceived need is an actual need: there is no difference between them. Meeting survival and safety needs is essential to attracting and keeping good workers. The ability to meet higher level needs also affects these leadership steps, but more importantly, meeting these needs will spell the difference between a good and great organization. The dichotomy of higher level needs in today's multi-generational workplace is that, while needs exist for all people, the means of meeting those needs are often diametrically opposed from one generation to the next.

The first high level need is a need for social belonging and love. For the Silent Generation, this need is often fulfilled by membership in the many organizations and clubs that sprouted after World War II. The workplace itself can also provide a sense of belonging. It's also important to note that the Silent Generation feels strong family ties and a sense of neighborhood, much as the GI Generation before them. What is significant for this generation is that their need for socialization is fulfilled in the form of human contact and personal relationships.

In *Bowling Alone: The Collapse and Revival of American Community,* Robert Putnam details the decline in American social community. He points out that participation in everything from social clubs to informal card playing in the home has decreased over the last 30 to 40 years. He offers several possible reasons for this including the pressures of time and money as two income households become the norm and everyone's life seems to get busier and busier. He also mentions other influences such as mobility and the fact that small town America tends to be giving way to urbanization of the population. Of course technology seems to be a contributor as well.[4]

Boomers social belonging is tied very closely to the workplace. They spend a lot of time there and their competitive nature makes it essential for them to feel they belong in the hierarchy of the organization. The family as a source of social belonging is very difficult to define for this generation. Family bonds tend to be a little stronger with earlier Boomer cohorts, but to say family is not important to later cohorts is certainly not universally true. Boomers do tend to form social groups around similar professions and income classes. In the workplace, it's usually important for Boomers to be part of a team.

The younger generations are quite different. Xers grew up in a world that was becoming increasingly wired and they began to have social interaction electronically. They also seem to be more distrustful of older institutions, placing more social value in smaller groups of close friends. They also want a life that is more oriented around family and are willing to sacrifice what Boomers often consider critical work time, like weekends and late evenings. Sometimes Xers are written off from a social perspective in the workplace, labeled as non-conformist or even anti-social. From a Boomer perspective, they may appear that way, but they really aren't. Many Boomers feel that Xers are not good team players. In fact, some Xers believe that as well. But, I've found that Xers, like everyone else, generally want to be part of a team, especially a winning team. They may prefer to work alone, but that doesn't negate their belonging need; just changes how that need is satisfied. Some of the feeling that Xers aren't team players stems from the fact that many Xers aren't willing to sacrifice the rest of their lives for the organization. That doesn't mean they don't care, or don't want to be an integral part of the team, just that the workplace team isn't the only thing in their lives. Successful leaders must provide their Xers with real opportunities to contribute without expecting them to give up everything else for the team. I'll add one caveat to that. While Boomers might knock themselves out to appear to belong and be a valuable part of the team, primarily because they feel they must in order to compete against the legions of peers all fighting for the same promotion, Xers want to belong to something that is meaningful to them. Therefore, if the leader convinces the Xer that the team's mission is important and worthwhile, and that the Xer's contributions are critical, they will probably find the Xer to be just as dedicated as the Boomer, perhaps more so.

Millennials socialize on the internet. They email, instant message, and text their way through life, establishing a network of "friends" many of whom they may never have met in person. Even with those with whom they have a personal relationship, much of that communication will be accomplished through technological means. This is somewhat baffling to previous generations who are more accustomed, and comfortable, with face-to-face communication, or even letter writing. Millennials are a huge generation and, like Boomers, they want to succeed, even excel. Probably the hardest task for leaders is to introduce Millennials to the world of face-to-face communication while not disparaging their propensity for on-line interaction.

The next level of need is self-esteem. Many Silent and Boomer Generation members feel this term has received way too much attention. For those generations, self-esteem was something to be earned by hard work and honest living. Being good at their job and able to provide for a family helped the Silent Generation feel good about themselves. Boomer's self-esteem came from climbing the corporate ladder or earning raises and promotions: generally being recognized by authorities for doing a good job. For Xers, self esteem comes from a different place. While strong family life was a source of self-esteem for previous generations, Xers grew up in a decidedly different environment that didn't include that family cohesiveness. They are sometimes called the "me generation" (that title was also applied to Boomers at one time) and it is true that they are more likely to answer their own desires than the organization's needs which they may not understand. They derive self-esteem from their ability to meet their own needs and achieve success as they see it. Many Xers feel caught between the much larger Boomer and Millennial Generations and a concept like self-esteem is very difficult to define. Much has been written about how this generation feels left out or underappreciated which provides leaders with an opportunity to begin to satisfy the self esteem need. Treating Generation X workers as valuable individuals will go a long way towards meeting this need.

Millennials were taught self-esteem from a very early age. Often, feeling good about themselves took priority over actually learning in school or adhering to societal standards. This emphasis on self-esteem, with their natural ability to effectively use technology, makes them something of a leadership challenge. Many Millennials grew up in a world where everyone was supposed to win, so it's like being doused with cold water when they find that everyone doesn't always win and the organization is not about them. Leaders must help the Millennial employee win real victories, giving them opportunities to earn success, then reward them for their win. Also important is helping them learn to effectively interact with their coworkers on a personal level. To both Silent and Boomer Generations, and even Xers to some extent, Millennials appear rude. To understand why, remember that Millennials have grown up in a world where it is acceptable to use language forms older generations find objectionable, such as heavy use of acronyms and shortened words, blunt references to each other, and generally disparaging views and comments about authority. They appear rude to the older generations because, by the standards of those generations, they often are! So again, the leader's job is to help the new Millennial understand how to communicate. I'll discuss communication more in a little later.

The final level of need according to Maslow is self-actualization. He felt that many people never reach this level and those who do never completely satisfy this need. To be self-actualized is to be always seeking new opportunities and new levels of success. Interestingly, I find that the generation most likely to be self-actualized is Generation X. I believe that's because they have gone through life with a healthy skepticism while also feeling that they are their own best advocate. They seem to want to achieve a balance between work and personal life, but that doesn't mean they don't want to be successful. Xers want it their way, will set high goals, and are willing to do what is necessary to achieve those goals.

Many Boomers don't see Xers in that way. Since Xers aren't as likely to play the corporate ladder games that the Boomers grew up with, and because Xers do emphasize a more balanced life, Boomers often see them as lazy or unmotivated. That impression is definitely off base! In the near future, as Boomers start to leave the workplace in ever larger numbers and Xers become firmly positioned in leadership roles, we'll see a level of achievement for which many Boomers could have only dreamed.

For the Silent and Boomer Generations, self-actualization is more of an individual issue than a generational one. While Xers demonstrate a more cohesive example of a self-actualized group, the older generations do not. Many never saw a need to reach this level, living very contently while achieving a comfortable level and staying there. Some do strive to constantly improve and reach new heights though, especially for Boomers, this was often driven more by job competition than satisfaction of an individual drive and focus on a particular ability or personal development.

I have found it very difficult to define self-actualization among Millennials. They are a very large group, yet don't seem as driven to the corporate ladder as their Boomer predecessors. Their propensity for web-based socialization makes them a little difficult to understand as a group and many are still too young to have reached this stage. Millennials may tend to redefine self actualization. While a Boomer or Xer might think of self actualization as achieving their full personal potential, Millennials may come to understand it as achieving the ability to continuously impact society as a whole.

At the beginning of this chapter, I mentioned another Maslow theory: Eupsychian Management. Maslow provides an essential point for leaders to remember; specifically that motivation changes as people achieve higher levels of need. Young workers, with few skills and limited means will probably be motivated to meet physiological and safety needs, but once those needs are met, they will be motivated by opportunities to achieve more. The successful leader must strive to recognize when these motivational changes occur and be ready to meet the higher needs and further develop the worker. When leaders can do this, an organization will begin to enjoy much greater success!

This is especially critical with Generation X and Millennials. They expect leaders to be cognizant of their needs and when they begin to feel their leaders either aren't aware, or aren't concerned with their needs, they are very likely to seek other opportunities. That doesn't mean leaders must be constantly asking workers if they're happy or if they feel fulfilled. Rather, these generations expect leaders to make the effort to understand their needs, which is difficult for Silent and Boomer generations to understand, since they feel no one was ever too concerned with their higher level needs.

On the other hand, there are Xer leaders in today's workplace who also fail to grasp the needs of Boomer subordinates. For example, in one situation, an Xer failed to understand that a Boomer employee had knowledge and experience to contribute. The Boomer became quite frustrated when shut out of a process because the Xer felt that he, the Boomer, could not possibly understand and therefore had nothing to contribute, thus failing to consider the employees belonging or self esteem needs.

# Chapter 9
# How Do I Motivate Thee
# Let Me Discover the Ways

Understanding needs is crucial for successful leadership, but the leader must understand what motivates people to help them achieve those needs. As Maslow said, motivation will change as needs change. Motivation is a tricky subject though. How does a leader know what really motivates workers? Do workers themselves know what really motivates them? Though the various generations respond to different motivators, there are some basics that haven't changed much over the years and apply equally to all generations; however, they might need to be applied a little differently.

Are leaders responsible for motivating workers? That's a contentious question. There are some people who appear to be self-motivated. On the other hand, there are those who appear to need someone else to provide some sort of external motivation. That might be in the form of a check or perhaps the threat of discipline. In reality, motivation is something that comes from within the individual, so it's the leader's responsibility to find what an individual's motivation is. As we'll examine later, individual's motivational factors will vary between the generations.

Leaders first need to understand what motivational factors are. Frederick Herzberg developed and tested what he called the Motivation - Hygiene Theory in the 1950s and 1960s. He showed that there are factors which motivate people simply called motivators, and those that can cause dissatisfaction but, by themselves do not motivate workers, which he labeled hygiene factors.[1] Hygiene is an unfortunate label as these factors have nothing to do with health or brushing one's teeth. Rather hygiene factors refer to such things as the work environment and poor ergonomics, which can lead to employee dissatisfaction. Herzeberg's research showed that fixing these problems will not necessarily motivate the worker, but can remove barriers to motivation.

Herzberg's motivational factors are such things as a feeling of achievement, the necessary authority to do quality work, and advancement as recognition for good work. His studies showed that these factors were what caused workers to do superior work.[2] While leaders realized positive results when they applied motivators, it's important to note that improvements were greater when the dissatisfiers, the hygiene factors, were also addressed. By removing the dissatisfiers, leaders cleared the way for the motivators to have a positive effect.

I first learned of Herzberg's theories many years ago at the same time I learned of Maslow's Hierarchy of Needs. Since then I have continually observed that the motivational side of Herzberg's theory is inextricably linked to Maslow's Hierarchy because, in order to know what motivates a worker, a leader must understand that person's needs. This is what Maslow was expressing with his theory of Eupsychian Management. For instance, if a worker feels he or she is just struggling to survive, then they are more likely to be motivated by such things as salary and benefits. But, once that worker feels secure, they move to higher level needs and factors such as increased responsibility and being a valued member of a team become the primary motivators. There is also a less obvious connection between the Hierarchy of Needs and hygiene factors, or dissatisfiers. These hygiene, or environmental, factors can be related to a person's safety which is a lower level need. If a worker doesn't feel safe on the job, either physically or mentally, they will not respond well to motivational factors.

It is tempting to create laundry lists of motivators and tell leaders to pick two from Column A, one from Column B, etc. That doesn't work, especially in today's dynamic workplace. Leaders must learn what will motivate each worker. Likewise, leaders must be on the lookout for, and actively pursue, those things that act as dissatisfiers. This is where leaders earn their pay as everyone is different and will find different things dissatisfying.

As I said, motivation is not all that different between generations. That's because, regardless of age, people are people and the human responds to certain things. One thing that is common among all age groups is the desire to be treated with respect.[3] It's amazing how many leaders don't understand this! What is different among the generations is the effect of not treating workers with respect. While Silent and Boomer Generation people might grumble and continue working, though certainly not producing at anywhere near their potential, Xers and Millennials might very well walk. These generations were not raised to believe they had to endure such things.

Being on a winning team is a great motivator. There seems to be an innate need in all humans to win. One has only to examine the huge industry that is college and professional sports (and even children's sports programs) to see that competition seems to be a central tenet of the human spirit. I have observed a little less of this, at least overtly, in the Millennial Generation; however, I know that spirit is still there, though perhaps manifested a little differently. Observe a Millennial playing a video game. They certainly aren't striving to lose! There are some interesting differences though. Silent Generation members want to be part of an effort to help the organization win. They strive to contribute to overall success. Boomers, who developed such a competitive spirit, wanted to win, but they also wanted the win to achieve personal success for their own advancement.

Xer's and Millennial's desire to win is no less strong, but they may need to be shown how the win benefits them. As more and more Millennials enter the work force and find themselves competing with each other as well as Xers and Boomers who have delayed retirement, their attitude toward winning may become more like their Boomer grandparents.

Another motivator that I've found to be common among the generations is a feeling of importance and trust. There seems to be a human desire to feel needed and be considered an important part of something. What has changed through the years is the need to more clearly define a worker's importance. The earlier generations did not pay much attention to this sort of thing, though they still wanted to be recognized as an important part of an operation or enterprise. A component of this feeling is a belief that they are trusted by the boss. When I speak to people from the GI or Silent Generations, they usually tend to downplay what they did but there is an underlying pride that they were an important part of making it happen and that the boss trusted them to do the right thing at the right time. These generations were raised to not toot their own horns.

Boomers had no such reluctance. With such a large group of competitors, they were less shy about wanting people to know about their contributions. Their recognition often came in the form of promotion or material rewards and from that they drew the inference that they were important and the boss trusted them. Now Boomers sometimes have trouble with the younger generation's seeming need for more overt recognition of their contributions. Rewards are still important, but often a more obvious approach may be required.

Xers have a somewhat skeptical view of the world in general and the workplace in particular. Explaining to them how their contributions are important is necessary, but they have to believe the boss believes in their importance; a difficult and sometimes unfamiliar standard for Boomers to meet. Xers can sniff out insincerity and will quickly turn off input they feel isn't real. The true motivator is not a pat on the head but a real understanding that the worker is important to success and the boss really does know that. For Xers, the issue of trust cuts both ways. They want to know that the boss trusts them; but, they also are more likely to let the boss know whether that trust is reciprocal. This can be a little disconcerting to earlier generations who are not used to what they would consider to be insubordination.

Millennials are probably more like Boomers in this regard. They too want to feel important, but they don't really need a lot of talk about it. In fact, they will respond best to the recognition that they know what they're doing. Unfortunately a problem arises here as the Millennial Generation doesn't approach things like their older supervisors. Recognition of their importance and trust in them might best be demonstrated by listening to their ideas and suggestions, while also showing an appreciation of their skills and abilities.

Though the methods of implementation may be different, I've found that people of all generations want to feel their knowledge and experience is appreciated and that the boss trusts and accepts them as an important part of the organization. A few years ago, I was given responsibility for leading a large organization and my leadership team was comprised of people from three generations, Boomers, Xers, and Millennials. The organization had experienced some problems prior to my arrival as their previous boss was one who felt he had all the answers and didn't need a lot of input. As a result, this leadership team had developed a belief that they had nothing much to contribute and that their input and expertise was not really trusted. I took an opposite approach, explaining that they were the experts and in order for the organization to fix its problems and move forward, I would need them to take responsibility for their own areas. One of the younger members of the team then asked me, "But will you listen to us?" I was a bit taken by surprise at this question, but as I looked around the room, I saw heads nodding and general agreement with his plea. My answer was that, not only would I listen, I needed and expected their input and would take it very seriously. I also told them that while I would carefully consider what any of them said, that didn't mean I would blindly implement their suggestions. About a year later I asked the same group if they felt I was listening to them. They agreed that I was and they appreciated the trust placed in them and in their critical contributions to our success.

What about those dissatisfiers? These too have changed with the generations. Though studies have shown that increased compensation isn't always a motivator, insufficient compensation can certainly be a dissatisfier. That much transcends the generations, since that compensation is what leads to satisfaction of basic survival needs.

Herzberg's studies were conducted when the GI and Silent generations were prominent and some Boomers were just beginning to enter the workforce. He talked of dissatisfiers like poor lighting. At that time, workplace safety was not the issue it is today, but was definitely a dissatisfier, preventing workers from completely meeting the basic need for safety. Reaction to dissatisfiers was quite different at that time. Leadership was often not as enlightened as it is today, so fixing dissatisfiers was seldom at the top of anyone's list of priorities.

As Boomers became more prevalent in the workplace, the nature of dissatisfiers changed. While those things identified in Herzberg's studies were still important, such things as not having access to symbols of status (like the corner office) or opportunities for promotion and more impressive titles became more common dissatisfiers.

Xers turned the whole issue on its head. They found the long hours and hard work ethic of the Boomers to be very dissatisfying and many have rejected it completely. They are more interested in balancing work with other aspects of life. They also often find the strict formality so common in large organizations to be restrictive and oppressive. They want a lot more freedom than their predecessors. I've found that Xers often reject the more formal business attire common in the workplace and that they are more comfortable in an informal setting.

Millennials, being the wired (or maybe wireless) generation want technology available to them: and they want it to be the best and most up-to-date. Inability to fully utilize their tech-savvy brains can lead to frustration and great dissatisfaction. Like Xers, they want informality in dress and relationships, but they aren't as adamant about it. Millennials also have problems with the way many organizations operate, especially when they see insistence on certain ways of communicating or what they see as slow or inefficient ways of accomplishing a task.

Just as a leader should strive to learn what motivates workers, he or she must also work towards an understanding of the things that dissatisfy the workers. For Boomers, removing these impediments, when possible, will help them respond more favorably to motivators. Again, the removal of dissatisfiers is not a motivator, but rather clears the way for motivators to be effective.

For Xers, dissatisfiers can have a consequence that wasn't as common with earlier generations. This generation is more willing to move on, as in find another job, and if there are enough issues, they may well do that. Conversely, it may be more difficult for leaders to make the changes necessary to remove dissatisfiers. For instance, many Boomers have become accustomed to making their work a central part of their lives, often to the exclusion of other things. Xers generally want to work hard, but then move on to family or hobbies after work. The conflict comes when the Boomer boss wants to work those long hours to meet a deadline and the Xer doesn't. The Boomer may not be able to meet the Xers desire to knock off at quitting time. A smart leader will help the Xer understand why the extra time is needed, and then will ensure the worker is given some other time off to compensate. More importantly, the leader can work to reduce or even eliminate the need for the overtime.

Millennials are entering the workforce at an interesting time. Many of them started when unemployment was very low but shortly after they began working as adults, the nation hit a serious recession with accompanying high unemployment. Since the Millennial Generation is even larger than the Baby Boom Generation and because Boomers are staying on the job longer, Millennials may find themselves in a precarious situation. Though I've found them to be like Boomers in some ways, their ability for parallel thinking and propensity for living an on-line life changes the equation in regard to dissatisfiers. Not having the latest and greatest tech gadgets may seem almost minor to previous generations, but to Millennials such a shortfall can affect their basic way of thinking. This may be classed as a dissatisfier, but it's a problem that can seriously degrade their effectiveness. Other dissatisfiers, such as not being able to use their normal truncated vernacular have more normal results. Millennials have generally shown a desire to comply when given good explanations and a chance to learn the new ways. They may be a little frustrated, but that usually doesn't stop progress. As a side note, leaders do have to work a little harder to help Millennials learn to deal with frustration, something they haven't had as much experience with as other generations.

When working with Millennials, leaders should make every effort to understand the dissatisfiers but not necessarily rush to fix them. In some cases, the worker's dissatisfaction is the result of a lack of understanding or a mistaken belief that what is bothering them needs to be changed. These people were raised in a world that often seemed to cater to them and so the leader must strive to help them adapt to a world that isn't necessarily going to accommodate their every need. Caution though! Remember, members of the Millennial Generation see things much differently than previous generations and what they might be expressing as a dissatisfier, upon closer examination, may really be an opportunity for a major positive change for the organization that had not been previously considered,

Of course, fixing dissatisfiers usually involves one, and sometimes both of two things: money and changing culture. No organization has enough money to address every problem that bothers every worker. The leaders challenge is to figure out what is worth the expenditure of precious resources and for those that fall below the cut line, make sure workers understand why the problem isn't fixed and what the plan is for the future. This is especially important for the younger generations. Though it doesn't remove the dissatisfier, when workers see that a leader has seriously addressed those things, and has a plan to continue addressing them, the impact of the dissatisfier is significantly reduced.

Fixing some dissatisfiers often involves changing the organization's culture. In this case the leader must consider whether the change is really beneficial. There is much to be said for organizational culture, but sometimes leaders hang on to cultural icons of the past for which younger generations see no purpose. A common example is business dress which has become decidedly less formal for younger generations, while many of the older generations still cling to a business suit as the standard. It's true however, that some cultural norms may be necessary and while they don't make sense to some workers, they still serve a purpose. While Boomers are much more accepting of these cultural norms, Xers are not. Leaders should sit down with their Xer workers and seriously discuss the dissatisfier. Learn what bothers the worker and have them suggest changes. There's a good chance that they will have seen something that wasn't obvious before and perhaps a change is possible that will satisfy the workers without drastically changing the culture. Or maybe the culture does need to be changed. Either way, Xers like to be instrumental in the change process and they appreciate leaders who are willing to give them an honest chance to make improvements. If a successful change is made, make sure to recognize the worker's contribution.

Chances are Millennial workers will have the greatest number of cultural dissatisfiers. That's to be expected since the organization is probably much different than what they experienced growing up. For leaders of Millennials, dealing with these dissatisfiers will be challenging, requiring patience and resilience. Leaders should understand that Millennials are usually not trying to be difficult (not that other generations are) but in many cases truly don't understand. Careful counseling by an enlightened leader will help them better understand life in the organization and will help make at least some dissatisfiers go away. As with Xers, listen carefully to the Millennial's complaint as they may see something with new eyes that would be an improvement. If so, make them part of the change and again, don't hesitate to give credit where it's due.

# Chapter 10
# I Know You Heard What You Think I Said
# But Did I Say What You Think You Heard?

Communication is one of the most difficult and volatile issues in the workplace. Miscommunication has caused many problems and led to loss of income, profits, and even lives. This is certainly not a generational issue, it happens across the entire spectrum of age groups, both between those groups and even within them. How to deal with communication issues is definitely related to the generational groups. Human interaction has changed over the years and is one of the most prevalent causes of problems in the workplace.

In the earlier generations, the boss issued an edict and subordinates responded. They were cautious about asking questions because questions might be interpreted as implying that the boss was not clear or that the subordinate was questioning their authority. Today that seems a little silly, though there are still vestiges of that in some organizations. There is another fact about GI, Silent, and Boomer Generation communication. They didn't have computers, cell phones, or Blackberries! We sometimes forget that these are relatively recent additions to the communications arsenal. These generations grew up with the written and spoken word and the writing was actually done with a pen or pencil on a piece of paper. For more formal presentation, they used a tool that some in the later generations may have only heard about; a typewriter. The significance should not be missed. These generations had to be able to express themselves in written and face-to-face communication and improvement of that skill provided an avenue to success.

With the computer age came a drastic change in communication and with it the need for a new set of skills. Interestingly, the earlier generations adapted to computers and cell phones fairly well, but the later generations did not see the need to adapt these technological capabilities to the normally accepted styles of communication. And that's where the generation gap widened. Supervisors from earlier generations learned to write on the computer much as they had with pen and paper, but they still used accepted grammatical rules. Later generations didn't see a need for that and different styles, such as omitting capital letters, or using all capital letters, or shortening words beyond recognition (for older people anyway) became common. There are two interesting observations from this new trend. First, written documents are much more likely to contain misspelled words, even though there are now easy to use tools to correct at least some spelling errors. Second, the same people who can't seem to produce a properly formatted document (by older generation standards) are wizards with computer programming and the language of web site construction, which is extremely precise.

All this results in a singularly difficult dilemma for the leader. Communication in the workplace is critical to organizational success, but there seems to be a wide chasm between the generations. When confronted with this problem, I suggest to leaders that they do not make it a bigger issue than it is, especially in everyday conversation. At the same time, it's important for leaders to maintain the standards that are important. So what's important? That's hard to say. When I submit articles or write books, editors expect me to adhere to certain grammatical styles. But, when receiving informal reports from subordinates, I certainly didn't send them back with corrections. I felt those people had more to do than worry about where the commas go in such informal communication. I know of other Boomer supervisors though, who insist on perfect communication every time. While that may be a noble cause, it's generally not worth the effort.

The most difficult relationship is with Millennials. While all the other generations had at least some requirement to write in what might now be considered old fashioned styles, Millennials have embraced such tools as email, instant messaging, and text messaging since their inception and are comfortable with the corresponding truncated words and thoughts. That works fine for them and they don't see why it doesn't work for everyone else as well. Though a difficult situation at best, leaders must help younger workers understand that there is a different standard for professional communication. I've found that most Millennials will adhere to those standards when it is explained to them; however, there's a problem. It often isn't just a matter of telling them to write correctly because they may not know how. Indeed, it may be necessary to teach a little business writing to give them the tools they need.

Methods of communication have experienced a giant change. Where previously written communication was often in the form of a bulletin, or the ubiquitous memo posted on the bulletin board, new generations are ushering in social media. Use of devices by conference or seminar attendees is an interesting development that demonstrates how technology has changed basic etiquette. While it is considered rude to talk during such a meeting, it has become commonplace to send text messages about what's going on. Use of social media sites (Twitter and Facebook are extremely popular at the time of this writing) allows attendees to tell the world that the speaker or leader is great, or terrible, or missing the point, or boring them, or any other comment they wish to make. Once sent, these comments become part of the permanent database that is the internet. A study by Towers Watson shows that U.S. companies are greatly increasing their electronic communication while decreasing print communication. Use of social media is expected to increase in 41% of the companies surveyed.[1]

Another significant factor that appears in the Towers Watson study is that companies are working harder to communicate not just changes, but the reason for changes and anticipated results. Though concentrating on such things as compensation and benefits, they go beyond those areas to such basics as corporate values. Statistics showed that although U.S. companies did well in all surveyed categories of communication, there was definitely room for improvement with at least 1/3, and sometimes over 1/2 of employee's responses indicating communication was not sufficient.[2] The greater significance here is that not too long ago, this would not have even been something of importance to study. New generations are less willing to be left in the dark, and they expect information to be provided in a way they're familiar with. That's rubbing off on earlier generations who are learning to adopt more technical means of communicating with subordinates, peers, and bosses.

The other critical form of communication is speaking. Many people in the workplace will never have to perform any serious writing chores but everyone speaks and I've found that there is much less difference in the generations in this regard. I believe that's because speaking is something first learned in the home where initial skills are cemented long before any formal education can have an effect. Earlier generations were often taught to speak only when spoken to and then to express themselves in a courteous and respectful manner. This translated well into the workplace where there was a definite hierarchical structure. Today, some children are taught to speak clearly, respectfully, and concisely while others are not.

Xers often have a different approach. As many grew up with influences from everywhere but home, they don't necessarily have the same sense of respectful speaking familiar to older generations and are more likely to say what they're thinking with no sugar coating. Leaders will need to get used to this as it is a deeply ingrained tendency and very difficult to change. This may not be all bad. The Xers, and especially Millennials, often think previous generations are not clear and beat around the bush too much. They don't see the need, or utility for the tactful approach taught to earlier generations and would rather come right out and tell you what they're thinking. For the leader with a thicker skin, who's willing to listen, this isn't all bad, as they can learn things about their organization that might otherwise have remain suppressed.

Many people believe Millennials can't speak at all. That's true in some cases but is too sweeping a generalization. Growing up with many forms of on-line social media has resulted in development of what is really a different language. When using technological means to communicate with each other, they use short text and radically truncated words. When they have to communicate by speaking to people unfamiliar with their vernacular, there will be problems. Some of this communication problem is also driven by the fact that Millennials are often uncomfortable outside their own small social groups. Leaders must help them learn to communicate effectively. Unfortunately, there are some leaders who interpret this communication problem as inability or unwillingness to work or become part of the team. It is more productive to view such apparent anti-socialism as a type of shyness.

One of the most important communication skills related to speaking is listening. I use the word in an older context that implies not only hearing but also understanding. I don't find a particular difference in generations in regard to hearing what others say. Some people are good listeners and some are not. Unfortunately, leaders often do not use good listening skills when dealing with workers, often causing or at least exacerbating otherwise minor problems. The affect of this lack of listening skill is where the generational issues arise.

The earlier generations might have been upset that the boss didn't listen, but there probably wasn't a whole lot they could do about it in the strict hierarchal structure of the time. As Boomers became a dominate force in the workplace, listening skills improved somewhat as they tried to fix perceived (and often very real) problems they saw in the corporate world. However, the mass of people competing for jobs and promotions limited their potential actions. That Boomers would emerge as better listeners would be a logical expectation, but I haven't found that to be entirely true. This raises a problem with the younger generations.

Many parents have heard children complain, "You just don't listen to me" or, "You don't understand." Likewise, every parent has probably said to a child that they "better start listening". That's a situation that is now becoming common in the workplace. Earlier generations sometimes complain that Xers don't listen to their instructions, advice, admonitions, etc. On the other hand, Xers feel the boss doesn't listen to their ideas, complaints, issues, etc. Both are often correct; at least to some degree. But while Boomers may have felt powerless to address the issue, Xers do not. They are much more outspoken about what makes them unhappy and they are more likely to make employment decisions based on those feelings.

Millennials may or may not express their discontent to the leader, but they very well may take action based on their perception of whether the boss listens. They are also very likely to tell their on-line social network about the problem which means what used to be issues that stayed inside the organization can now be quickly be aired for the whole world (and potential customers and clients) to see.

It's obvious then that the leader must listen (and understand). All generations want to be heard and know their input is taken seriously. If they believe they received a fair hearing, most employees will respond positively. When the boss doesn't listen, the impact can be disastrous, for the very people who will become the leaders of tomorrow.

# Chapter 11
# It Takes All Kinds
# Generations and Diversity in the
# Workplace

When the word diversity is mentioned, the spotlight is usually clearly focused on race and gender with emphasis on sensitivity to everyone's feelings and the eradication of personal prejudices. This is a noble goal and great progress has been made, but the differences in the generation's experiences plays a major, and often little considered role. Successful leaders need to keep two things in mind. First, our society has made great strides in race and gender relations since the early years of the Silent Generation; but, while on a societal level there has been much improvement, it is very difficult to change individual beliefs and teachings ingrained from early childhood. Second, diversity cannot be just about race or gender. Each person is an individual. Though we tend to lump people into categories, in this case by the year of their birth, we must still accept that not everyone will fit within the expected margins. The true beauty of the human is that each one brings something a little different.

The Silent Generation grew up in a time when the overwhelming majority of the nation's middle and upper class were Caucasian. The rest of the population lived predominantly in the lower class brackets. It's important to remember that the first cohort of the Silent Generation was born between 60 and 65 years after the end of the Civil War and the end of slavery in the U.S. That's approximately the same period as between the end of World War II and publication of this book, a period of time too short to have erased memories and individual prejudices. Though the Civil War marked the end of slavery, it certainly didn't mark the end of discrimination or individual prejudice. Professional and societal integration would not come for many more years and in the mean time, much of that generation was steeped in the bias and prejudice that was very often an institutional constant of the day. To be fair, this generation has come a long way as a group and the systemic discrimination of the past is rapidly passing as a bad memory.

Gender issues have not passed quite as easily. As discussed in Part I, there are still issues of gender equality that need work. Here though, the Silent Generation grew up in a world where women were generally not expected to work, or if they did, only at certain "pink collar" jobs. World War II changed that, if only temporarily, and introduced women to the workforce in a grand way. Though large numbers of working women returned to the home after the war, they had tasted another life and change would come much more rapidly.

As the Boomers began to take center stage, they faced these issues head on. Led by what were often considered radicals from the Silent Generation, they rejected the idea that skin color was an indicator of intelligence or ability and Boomer women attacked the workforce with a vengeance. They rejected their parents and grandparents views of race and fought for equality.

They made great strides, but didn't end racism or gender inequality.

It's impossible to quantify bias or prejudice. Some people would report their feelings and beliefs honestly, but most would not. Boomers, who may have rejected the prejudice of their forebears, still grew up in a world where that prejudice continued to be strongly held and often institutionalized. Still, much of the improvement has occurred during the Boomers time and they generally consider themselves enlightened on these issues.

Xers grew up in this more enlightened world and are less likely to hold ingrained prejudices. They do see continued problems though and are sworn to fix what they feel their parents did wrong; much like Boomers. The time of race riots had, for the most part, passed and while there was still some unrest from time to time, the issue had settled considerably. Of real significance was the improvement in treatment of minorities, the end of segregation, and the rise of true integration. What Xers see as problems now, while important, are not the serious issues of the past. The Xer Generation was too young to remember the race riots and civil unrest of the 1960s and early 1970s. That isn't to say they aren't aware of that period in American history. They still take the issue very seriously and will continue to strive for full equality in all aspects of life. One indicator of the level of change was reported in a 2005 Gallup poll which found that acceptance of interracial dating has increased considerably through the years, with Boomers showing approximately 35% more acceptance than their parents, Xers showing a 26% increase over Boomers, and

Millennials showing a 23% increase over Xers. The study indicates that Millennials may be even more enlightened on race than Xers.[1]

I use this issue of racial acceptance as an example of how such attitudes can change across generations. It also demonstrates that at least outwardly, things can change even when the majority of the generation may have been raised to think differently. It also demonstrates that the work of one generation benefits the next, even if the younger generation doesn't understand how much of a change has actually occurred.

This issue isn't dead though and while Xers will continue to push for what they see as a continued need for change, Millennials will simply expect it to be a non-issue.

When studying the various generations, diversity has another, more far-reaching aspect. Regardless of race, gender, or any other factor of life, each person in the workplace is different. A leader must recognize these differences. But how? More than ever, it's important to know the workers. As we have discussed, the leader needs to know what motivates them.

Another form of diversity, which is really the focus of this book, is generational diversity. As the Baby Boom Generation ages, there is talk of age discrimination, or ageism in the workplace. At the same time, some members of the Silent Generation have decided to return to work, at least part-time, making generational diversity a complex issue. The job search site for executive level candidates, *TheLadders.com,* discusses this at length and suggests applicants should work to deemphasize age when writing resumes and interviewing.[2]

Generational diversity is not just about ageism, but rather the need to relate to members of each generation as individuals; understanding their motivations while, at the same time, allowing for their differences. Each generation really comes from a different world. What the Baby Boomers experienced in their early years is almost unfathomable to Millennials. The early years of Generation X presented challenges for that group that have not been faced by any other. The Silent Generation, which still holds sway over some of the most senior levels of corporate America, was raised in a world that is quite unrecognizable to the other generations. When all these different worlds come together, there's bound to be conflict, or at least misunderstanding. Dealing with this is a two way street. While it may be difficult for Baby Boomers to understand Millennials, they must put forth the effort. By the same token, it is difficult for Millennials to understand the motivations, or even the thought process of the other generations, but they must try. The result will be a greatly improved work situation for all concerned and a much better flow of ideas.

But, do all these generational differences really equate to a significant diversity problem in the workplace? A study by AchieveGlobal seems to indicate that the problems commonly associated with the different generations may not be as prevalent as common knowledge would indicate. Their findings agree with my own observations in many different types of organizations. The survey indicates there is not much concern for age differences or feeling that age influences how people behave or what they desire. Interestingly, the one generation that did not completely agree with the others was the Silent Generation which was a little more likely to say that age did make a difference.[3] The obvious lesson here is that leaders should take care not to read too much into generational differences or create problems where none may actually exist.

But, even though the generational diversity may not have the significance some have assigned to it, there remains the fact that people are different and they come from different experiences. It seems each generation feels at least somewhat misunderstood and underappreciated and wants the other generations to just listen and appreciate their experience, knowledge, or just what they have to say. Most of us want the other person to change; we shouldn't have to.

# Chapter 12
# Why Should I Change?
# Why Can't You Change?

Leadership tends to be very personality driven and people tend to reflect previous leaders when they take on a leadership role themselves. Boomer era leaders grew up at a time when an authoritarian style was more common; but, also when some were becoming more enlightened. Until fairly recently, leaders did not concern themselves too much with the idea of knowing individual subordinates and understanding their needs and motivations. They just issued orders and expected obedience. That's the way the Silent and GI Generation bosses did it and so that's what they learned. But, there were those who studied leadership in the mid-twentieth century and began to suggest a more participative style of leading. As some leaders saw that those styles were more effective, there began a general shift towards the newer methods. Of course, that wasn't universally true. In some industries, those who were uncomfortable relinquishing the more authoritarian styles felt threatened and tended to hunker down and adopt a defensive posture.

Another problem is that many Baby Boomers worked hard their whole lives to reach the point where they were making the decisions and issuing the orders and they saw new ideas about leadership styles as threatening everything they worked for. So, when a new generation comes along with different, sometimes radically different, ideas and work ethics, the older generations don't always want to hear it.

On the other hand, Xers and Millennials grew up in a very different world and expected not only a different leadership style, but a whole new work environment. The Silent and Baby Boom Generations were used to a certain status quo, while Xers and Millennials were more used to getting what they wanted and making their own decisions at a much earlier age, thus setting the stage for conflict.

So, who changes? Most of the literature written by Boomers indicates they have done great things and other generations need to realize that and change their ways. The literature written by Xers tends to show that they have had a difficult life up to now and, though the other generations don't understand them, they have the answers to a better world and other generations need to realize that and change their ways. There isn't much real literature yet by Millennials, but one can certainly find a considerable body of their musings on the internet indicating they are the only ones who really get it and everyone else is just wrong or confused and need to change their ways. Interestingly, I've found very few examples of one generation speaking well of another.[1]

One thing that's common, and correct, is that everyone needs to change. We no longer live in a "my way or the highway" type of world. Everyone must be willing to see where changes are needed. At the same time, everyone must understand that it isn't just the other guy who needs to change.

Let's look at some specific examples.

## Work Hours

Boomers often look at the work day as starting early and ending late, with the occasional addition of a weekend. Family is important, but work is what supports the family's life style. Xers think family is important too. In fact, it's more common for them to cut the overtime short for the family. This attitude confounds Boomers and in their eyes, makes Xers look a little less committed. Are they? Remember that Boomers faced two big issues in their formative working years. One was the GI and Silent Generation bosses who had grown up in a world of unquestioning obedience and were not very open to radical change from their Boomer underlings. The other was the large numbers in the Boomer generation, all competing for jobs and the corner office. So, along came Xers who didn't have as great a need to compete on the job and who grew up with the job obsessed Boomers. It wasn't that they didn't want to work or succeed, they just didn't want to do it the way their parents had. Here's the interesting thing. There doesn't seem to be a decrease in productivity where Xers are a large part of the workforce.

Then along came the Millennials. Like Xers, they aren't all that interested in the constant 60+ hour work weeks. That doesn't mean they don't want to be successful. Even more than Xers, they have a very low tolerance for bureaucracy. They have a different and often better way of handling and processing information and are most likely the key to increasing the efficiency of the organization, allowing for a more balanced life.

Are Boomers going to change and relax a little? Some will but the majority probably won't. What they can do is let Xers, and Millennials begin to shape the future with a more balanced life style. They'll do that by examining rules, policies, and procedures that have often become common and unquestioned, creating a more efficient workplace. Boomers must not take this change as a personal assault, but realize the change will probably increase efficiency. On the other hand, Xers and Millennials must understand that they are seeking change in areas that a Silent or Boomer Generation member may be personally invested in. The best approach is to carefully explain a new method and its advantages without denigrating the old system or method.

Though I've referenced Xers and Millennials together here, they are distinctly different. Xers are closer to Boomers than they might want to admit in this regard and will likely bristle at the Millennials tendency to expect things to be in their favor. On the other hand, Xers are more likely to bluntly state what they want with less regard for corporate etiquette.

Loyalty

A common refrain concerning Xer and Millennial workers is that they have no job loyalty and will flit from one job to the next without a thought. While there is some truth to that, it isn't quite as common as the stories would have us believe. It's important to remember that these generations approach the workforce from a very different point of view than the Silent or Boomer Generations did. As noted before, there has been a significant change in work attitudes from the Silent and Boomer Generations to the Xer and Millennial Generations. Various reasons can be cited, but these changes reflect a change in society itself. A "family man" of the 1950s worked long hours to support his family and put food on the table. The fact that he was absent from the home for most of the day, and usually tired by evening, was considered a badge of honor. His children saw that Dad wasn't home a lot and vowed that when they went to work it was going to be different. Those noble thoughts quickly ran into reality and those kids, the Boomers, grew up to discover they had to work just as long and hard as Dad did in order to move ahead at the office.

Boomers quickly adapted to those long hours, not to mention the nice things success could buy. Instead of being home more, they may actually have found even less time for family. The first cohorts of that generation produced Generation X, and many promptly farmed them out to day care, after school programs, soccer coaches and whatever else would keep them busy.

As Generation X grew up, they too said this wasn't to be their life; but they were more successful, perhaps owing to the support of parents into their adulthood. Even though the 1980s and 1990s were primarily affluent times, Xers tend to view those decades as less than wonderful. As Xers were already approaching their adult years with a suspicious eye, these problems served to reinforce a somewhat apprehensive view of their future. They did not see corporate America as a particularly safe place, nor did they feel it was wise to place exclusive trust in any one organization.

These factors all tend to define the generation's loyalty to an employer. The Silent Generation grew up in the time of "The Company Man" where employees felt an allegiance to employers. Switching jobs was not common. That isn't to say they necessarily liked those jobs, but stayed on for the stability the job offered. They were loyal to the company because that's what was expected and it worked best for them.

Boomers were distrustful of "the establishment," but quickly found that same establishment provided the jobs that put food on the table. Reaching middle age, Boomers also realized that they had to work hard and compete in order to get ahead, while at the same time beginning to truly appreciate the benefits the establishment, and higher pay, had to offer. In many ways, Boomers put the distrust of their early years aside and gave a certain amount of loyalty to the company (though not quite as much as their parents) because that worked best for them.

Generation X did not invent distrust of their elders or the establishment under which those elders had prospered, but they haven't lost it either. They are much more likely to move on if they don't feel they're getting what they need, or if they see an opportunity to improve their own skills. That doesn't necessarily mean they are disloyal to the company, just that company loyalty may be second to their own desires. This is a very important point for leaders! Though much is written about Xer's tendency to change jobs at the drop of a hat, they don't all do that. A leader who treats their Xer employees with respect and strives to give them challenging work and opportunities to further their skills will be much less likely to lose them.

Much of the current research on Millennials focuses on their late teen years and so is not very helpful in determining how they will express loyalty, or lack of it, to a company. Remember that the Millennial Generation has grown up with a very self-centered view of the world. They are much closer to their parents and seem to be more respectful of establishment type authority than either their Boomer or Xer predecessors. A workplace that offers them an opportunity to use their skills and grow, while at the same time providing a support system, will probably find success.

## Communication and Business Etiquette

So much of business etiquette is related to communication that it's difficult to discuss one without the other. A leader must carefully examine ways to bring the generations together regarding these critical, and often volatile, subjects. For the Silent Generation, communication was often a one-way street. The boss decreed what was to happen and no one argued. Communication up the chain was much less common and could be hazardous to career success. The rules of etiquette tended to discourage disagreement and supported a fairly strict corporate hierarchy. Communication of that time was also much slower by today's standards. The telephone was really the fastest way to pass information, but the telephone was not portable or multi-functional.

This is the corporate world the Boomers entered. Certainly they became a full part of it, but that isn't to say they didn't shake it up some. They were more likely to communicate up the chain and were much more willing to ask questions and offer unsolicited opinions, though by later standards, they were still pretty tame. The pillars of corporate etiquette may have cracked a little bit, but they still held firm. The ubiquitous telephone began to be augmented by the advent of the pager. This one-way device could now tether a worker to the job around the clock and was the harbinger of things to come.

As Generation X entered the workforce, they brought with them a healthy skepticism and were more likely to express their doubts. They may not have accepted many of the older rules of etiquette, but at the same time they did not like Millennials violating the rules that Xers adhered to. Xers have proven to be more likely than previous generations to express themselves and question authority. Methods of communicating also changed drastically during this generation. They saw and embraced the advent of email, and later, cellular phones. This generation became fully connected and used these new tools to their advantage.

Then, along came the Millennial Generation. This generation has stood corporate etiquette on its head. Having grown up in a world that often encourages them to express their opinion, they are not shy about doing so in the workplace, and they expect their bosses to listen. They also brought something new to the workplace: their parents. Millennials have an unusually close relationship with their parents and those parents expected to be part of their children's adult lives. They will interject themselves in situations where previous generations would not have even considered intruding.[2] To further complicate matters, the Millennial Generation has taken communication to levels never considered by any other generation. Using truncated words and often ignoring commonly accepted grammar, they text their way through life and expect everyone else to keep up. However, leaders should be careful not to lump all Millennials together. A LexisNexis survey of legal and white collar professionals reports that 67% of Boomers and 68% of Xers feel that using a digital device in meetings is impolite compared to 57% of Millennials. Boomers and Xers found such use distracting by 68% and 64% respectively while only 49% of Millennials thought such use was distracting. When asked if such use was productive and efficient, 20% of Boomers and 33% of Xers said productive while 17% of Boomers and 30% of Xers said efficient. In comparison, 35% of Millennials said such use was both productive and efficient.[3] As would be expected, 69% of Boomers replied that personal Data Assistants (PDAs) and mobile phones contributed to a decline of proper workplace etiquette, 57% of Xers and 47% of Millennials agreed.[4] So, though more Millennials than Boomers or Xers thought use of new technologies was impolite, over half of them agreed and almost half felt such use was distracting.

An Xer financial advisor told me that he seldom uses email and doesn't text at all for business. He has found that using electronic means tends to stifle give and take of face-to-face communication and complained that there was a less reliable feedback loop with electronic communication.

Interestingly, in a 2006 Pew Research Survey, more Millennials that other generations, by 84% to 64%, felt technology made people lazy. But, 69% and 64%

respectively felt that technology could also make people more efficient.[5]

This data deserves a little thought. First, though the survey was of white collar and legal professionals, there seems to be agreement among a much larger cross-section of the working populace. As we've already discussed, the older generations are not as comfortable with higher technology invading the workplace, but successive generations have become more comfortable with the technological advances that occurred as they grew up. No surprise there. What is significant though is that the numbers show not everyone in older generations is adverse to new technology and. not everyone in younger generations is completely enamored with it either. And that's where etiquette and change meets the changing work ethic.

The Silent and Boomer Generations have been forced to at least accept new technology, even if the majority hasn't embraced it. Millennials, and to a somewhat lesser extent Xers have embraced technology and can't imagine life without it. Those in the older generations have had to change, while those in the younger generations have not. Millennials and Xers (again, possibly to a lesser extent) use this technological edge to skirt those things they see as impediments to their success. The leader's task is to leverage these new tools to increase efficiency while helping those who are uncomfortable with them learn to adapt. Millennials especially, must understand that expecting most Silent and Boomer Generation members to completely immerse themselves in technology is very similar to them asking Millennials to go without it. It would be very difficult!

Along the same lines though, those in the Silent and Boomer Generations must help the younger folks understand that the availability of nifty high tech tools does not negate the need for common courtesy and respect for each other. As the previously cited survey shows, this probably isn't that hard to do.

One more communication issue faces the leader. Quite simply, many members of the Millennial Generation have trouble separating computer language, such as short, terse text messages, or ungrammatical emails from commonly accepted business writing. It does not appear the world is ready for a text message type business report, so it may be necessary for a leader to provide a little more intensive training than was required in the past. To do so is certainly worth the time and effort.

### Planning for the Future

Some leadership experts are concerned about the potential for a coming leadership gap. There are some who feel Xers are not ready and perhaps not even capable of assuming leadership roles, and that Millennials are too self-absorbed to take on leadership roles. Nonsense! People will always emerge to fill leadership roles. It is the leader's job to help good workers become good leaders. There is legitimate concern that Boomers are beginning to leave the workforce and haven't properly trained and developed new leaders among Generation X. Whether real or not, this concern seems to be, in many cases, a self-fulfilling prophesy. Feeling that their Xer subordinates were not ready or capable of attaining leadership positions, Silent and Boomer Generation leaders often did not make the effort to move them forward. As they felt Xers were not ready, they withheld information. Without the flow of information Xers were at a disadvantage and did not realize the benefit of that knowledge. This creates a vicious cycle that tends to prove what was really a false premise to begin with.[6] Some Xers have exacerbated the situation by eschewing the "establishment" and rejecting a teamwork approach.

Leadership development must begin at the top of the organization, while emphasizing training and development for the lower levels of management. Often that means Silent or Baby Boom Generation leaders working to ensure organizations have an effective leadership development program in place. The difficulty members of these generations may have is that Xers, and to some extent Millennials, may not exhibit the same tendencies which made workers stand out in the past. However, closer examination will usually uncover the same type of drive and intensity. As noted earlier, workers may not have the same "work until they drop" type of approach to the job, but the potential leaders will still exhibit a strong work ethic, a desire to get things done right, and the ability to lead other people.

Leadership development has always implied some type of training. Unfortunately, that training hasn't always occurred. In fact, leadership training that starts at the earliest point in a leader's career and continues throughout is a serious shortfall in many organizations. While such training has always been critical, it is even more so today as there seems to be less skill for managing interpersonal interaction, especially with Millennials and younger Xers who have lived so much of their life on line, often at the expense of developing many actual face-to-face relationships. I have observed many younger people (usually in their 20s) who have great ideas but have no idea how to express themselves or relate to other people. Often, when these people are coached in human relationships they quickly begin to exhibit the kind of potential that makes them candidates for leadership.

All this may seem like more work for current leaders and in many cases it is, but it's a responsibility they must bear and besides, it can also be quite rewarding.

# Chapter 13
# How Do I Keep Them From Leaving?

Much has been written about Xers, and to a lesser extent Millennials being very job mobile. As I mentioned earlier, there is not yet truly accurate statistical data available (as in a long-term longitudinal study) to support that, but there is enough anecdotal evidence to make it a concern for leaders. How much of a concern is subject to some debate as data that is available is sometimes diametrically opposed. A 2006 Kelly Workforce study showed that job satisfaction was rated at 65% with 58% saying they were rewarded for a job well done. Respondents to the survey gave their bosses a 7.3 rating out of 10[1] which would indicate that the majority of workers seem to be satisfied with their current situation. The Bureau of Labor Statistics, Job Openings and Labor Turnover Survey reports that as many as 2 million workers quit their jobs every month. While that is normally less than 2 percent of the total workforce, it is definitely a very significant number and should be considered.[2]

In 1919, in anticipation of soldiers returning home from World War I, a popular song asked, "How Ya Gonna Keep 'Em Down On the Farm, After They've Seen Paree." Many leaders in the workplace find themselves asking a similar question. Reports indicate that 25% of employees have been in their current job for less than a year and 50% have been on the job less than 5 years.[3] A 2007

Center for Creative Leadership survey found that 60% of Boomers in the 1946 - 1954 cohorts would like to stay with their current organization until retirement while less than 30% of Xers in the 1977 - 1986 cohorts indicated the same constancy.[4]

Though earlier generations did change jobs, it was not nearly as common a practice as today when changing jobs is not considered unusual. In fact, I've found some companies don't give it a lot of thought, especially for their lower level employees. That's a rather short sighted view and a good leader must meet the issue of turnover head on. High turnover costs money. The actual cost varies from industry to industry and even from job to job, but is usually considered to be at least 50% and sometimes as high as 200% of the employee's annual salary. That's certainly enough to be concerned about! Once again, the solution seems to vary from one generation to the next. Retention is primarily an issue for the youngest two generations and there does seem to be a difference between them. Xers are the ones most commonly known for job switching. They have gone through life viewing the world as a very unstable place and tend to feel they must look out for their own interests. Seeking a level of security they saw with their parents, but which seems to have eluded them, they'll not hesitate to move on if they feel it's in their best interest. Silent and Boomer Generation bosses can understand the desire for security, but they also must understand that security to Xers does not necessarily mean a steady job with the same company. To Xers, security may mean adequate compensation, the opportunity for growth, and a balanced life. If their current situation doesn't offer that, then it's time to move on.

To keep Xers on the team, leaders should consider such things as job mobility within the company and work-life balance. Moving an employee to a different division will allow them to gain experience and develop a new skill set. Such internal movement will also provide the company with an employee who has a much broader view of the organization as a whole. Work-life balance is also a buzz phrase of Generation X. They don't want to be tied to the desk the way they perceive other generations to be. A smart leader will recognize that this isn't a desire to accomplish less, but to be more balanced in how they do the work. Leaders should keep in mind that Xers have two attributes that go a long way towards helping them achieve success without the long days and weekend work.

First, they are much less likely to be tied to the old corporate ways. They see the bureaucracy that has developed through the years as a hindrance. What's most important is that they see the bureaucracy at all! Many of the older generation are so used to it that it just doesn't register anymore. Xers are more likely to want to ignore or change those things that get in their way. A good leader will give serious attention to what their Xer employees are telling them.

Second, Xers are usually more technologically savvy and want to use the available tools to speed up work and be more efficient. Again, leaders should encourage their Xers to flex their innovative side. Xers and especially Millennials want to have the most current capabilities available. Though budgets may not always allow the newest and greatest gadgets, a cost-benefit review might reveal fiscal benefit for the upgrade.

There has been a big push to use more telecommuting to limit travel and time spent actually in the office. This can be an incentive for Xer employees; however, it isn't always the utopia it seems. Especially if the Xer is a parent, they may quickly learn that it's not possible to be as productive at home where there are multiple distractions just waiting to pounce.[5]

While Xers tend to be somewhat suspicious of the corporate world, Millennials see the world as their oyster. They are approaching the work world with enthusiasm; they really want to make a difference. In some ways they are very much like Boomers, but there are some significant differences. Most notably, as already discussed, as a whole they haven't learned to communicate as well as previous newcomers to the workplace. While that may not appear to be a retention issue, it can quickly lead to job dissatisfaction if not remedied. It appears that Millennials are more likely to expect to be loyal to a company rather than expecting to switch jobs as readily as Xers. However, leaders should not fall back on that as the solution to retention problems. Remember that Millennials are used to getting their way and if they feel they aren't getting a fair hearing they might well hit the road. Also, just like Xers (and really anyone else that a leader wants to take care of) leaders should consider lateral moves within the company to increase experience and knowledge. Remember that Millennials tend to be fast learners and many will appreciate the opportunity to increase their knowledge base.

Even more than Xers, Millennials are known for technology and are not likely to be impressed with a company that is satisfied with "the way we've always done it." With their ability to use the various computer tools available today, they can get a lot more done in a shorter period of time, so the investment has a considerable possibility for lucrative return.

A good example of the power, and problems, with technology and Millennials is social networking. This vehicle is how Millennials communicate with each other but it is also a point of friction with older generations who often don't understand how to use social media as a tool and so don't appreciate it. A survey by Price Waterhouse Coopers found that 92% of surveyed Millennials were members of a social media network.[6] I suggest that companies consider the power of social media to not only attract business, but also provide a new communications infrastructure that Millennials, and future generations are comfortable with.

Another factor stemming from the huge influence of social media that is sometimes very difficult for older generations to grasp is the impact it can have which the company may not even be aware of. There are two specific affects that leaders need to consider. First, if a Millennial is not happy about the company, the boss, or even the food in the snack bar, that discontent can very quickly become fodder for the web. If the dissatisfied employee is particularly gifted in writing or producing video, their complaints can quickly go viral[†], and put the company's name in a bad light.

Second, Millennials tend to judge things by what they see on the internet. If leaders want to attract young talent, they need to have a good, up-to-date website. One Millennial confided to me that he was not enthusiastic about working for a specific company because their website wasn't very good. Like it or not, every organization has an internet presence and, if judged insufficient, will be detrimental with this generation.

While Xers tend to be more cautious about commitment to a specific organization, Millennials are more likely to become the company people of the future; but with a twist. They want to use their talents to help the company succeed, but they also expect to receive some satisfaction in the process. Whereas Boomers were often willing to sacrifice some personal satisfaction because it was the price to pay for having a job and maybe getting ahead, Millennials are not.

The good news about the Millennial Generation is that they are a positive group and come to the workplace ready to be a part of the organization and ready to contribute. They will probably take a little more coaching than previous generations but the results will be worth the extra effort. When questioned on their situation and expectations in the Pew survey, 84% responded that their quality of life was excellent or good and 81% said their most important goal was to get rich.[7]

---

[†] "Going viral refers to a posting on the internet attracting large numbers of viewers. Once something "goes viral" on the internet, it may be seen by literally hundreds of thousands of people. It will also be beyond anyone's ability to stop or contain.

There is one thing that leaders need to remember when dealing with all generations. As the AchieveGlobal survey revealed, the number one workplace attribute among all generations is respect. This is the only attribute that was agreed on by all four generations surveyed.[8] Of course everyone wants to be shown respect, but members of the Silent and Boomer Generations were not always very vocal about the issue. Xers and Millennials are and will probably be even more so in the future. Unlike their predecessors, they will not suffer in silence!

# Chapter 14
# What Does The Future Hold And What Can I Do About It?

History is littered with the refuse of expert's predictions of what will happen in the future. There is no shortage of Nostradamus "wannabes" who claim to foresee gloom and doom or predict the demise of some long-standing social standard. Equally common are those who boisterously announce how some particular new technology will capture the market in a huge way. It's difficult to follow these predictions as most of them quickly fade into obscurity. However, it is important for leaders to have at least some thought for what the future might hold. So, in that vein, let's take a look at what the future of the generation issue might be.

There is already talk about the generation after the Millennials. The Millennial Generation is normally considered to end about the year 2000. Is that an accurate date? The divide between the GI Generation and the Silent Generation is well defined by service in World War II. Likewise the demarcation between the Silent Generation and the Baby Boom Generation is marked by the end of World War II. The line between Baby Boomers and Generation X is not so clear. Generally considered to be around 1964, there doesn't seem to be any particular event that marks the time. The Millennial Generation is normally considered to start in 1980. The year 1980 saw the election of President Ronald Reagan which signaled a change in the country's political leanings, and a desire for change in the economic situation; but the effects of that election did not actually occur for several more years. While the 2000 and 2001 period was certainly important in national history, I would expect the political and economic turmoil of 2008 - 2009 to represent a likely generational demarcation. Only time will tell where the next generation starts.

The march of technology seems to be, more and more, a defining factor when considering the generations. When I was young, I enjoyed hearing the stories of my grandparent's journeys to school on horseback, and about the brand-new automobile. These wonderful people seemed to be able to keep up with the changes in technology but towards the end of their lives, as those technological changes become more rapid, they seemed to reach the zenith of their ability to absorb them and what came after that point was mostly lost to them. I observe the same phenomenon in my parent's generation, though they have adapted better and it seems to have taken longer to reach the point of saturation. The Baby Boom Generation has stretched the limits even further but many seem unable, or unwilling, to keep up with the ever more rapid march of technology.

The world's adventures in space provide a good metaphor for how the generations have reacted to ever increasing technological progress. In the early GI Generation, the idea of space travel was science fiction and few gave it a lot of thought. By the end of the Baby Boom Generation and the beginning of Generation X space travel was a given and man would soon walk on the moon. By the end of Generation X and the beginning of the Millennial Generation space travel had moved to the outer reaches of our solar system and our eyes turned outward to the furthest expanses of space. In no less a way, technology will define the future generations.

So, what issues will leaders face in the future? To answer that question, let's look at some things that seem certain over the next decade or so. First is the sheer size of the Millennial Generation. At approximately 81 million, they are the largest generation in the nation's history. So far, this generation has proven to be very fruitful, producing over 41 million babies between 2000 and 2010[1]. If this birth rate continues through the year 2020, the generation following the Millennial's could be even larger. This means there will very likely to be too many workers for too few jobs. Let's examine why.

Baby Boomers are not retiring at the age most of the GI and Silent Generations did. If that trend continues, there will be significant numbers of Boomers in the workplace well into 2030. One of the reasons cited for Boomers staying on the job is that they just aren't ready to quit yet. There's no reason to believe Xers won't feel the same way as they age meaning they also will be in the workplace well into the future.

That means by the time the next generation hits the workplace, approximately 2020, they will be competing with three other generations. There is one other factor that has the potential to cause a serious problem. The United States entered a recession in 2008 that resulted in high unemployment rates. That recession, and the attending unemployment, has served to cause many companies to become more efficient, allowing them to produce the same, or even more with fewer employees so that when the economy enters a period of recovery, unemployment may not decrease as quickly, or as much, as has occurred after previous recessions.

That may sound like a great thing for leaders who will live in a strong employers market. In many ways the phenomenon is true today, but there are still many employees changing jobs because they don't like the leadership. I have no reason to believe that will change. Unfortunately, a market of this type tends to lead employers to adopt an attitude of "who cares, there are plenty more out there" when dealing with unhappy employees. That won't work! As we've seen, even in a period of economic distress, today's younger people are much more willing to move to another company, or just quit and wait a substantial amount of time for another job. Current generous unemployment benefits make that even more likely.

Another factor to consider is that even if there are plenty of replacements, it costs money to replace an employee. Leaders should consider the costs of recruiting and training, as well as the cost of having inexperienced workers. There are many other expenses that vary depending on the type of employee and the expertise required. The point is, replacing employees isn't free. Leaders should also consider that high turnover causes turmoil in the organization, which reduces efficiency.

As the various, and very different generations continue to converge on the workplace, there is a problem that today's leaders can avoid: a lack of future leaders. Some years ago, in many cases, Boomer leaders reached the conclusion that Xers would not be good leaders. This belief came from a fairly arbitrary observation of young Xers entering the workplace. Having worked with many of that generation, I can say beyond a doubt that they make fine leaders; when provided with the necessary training and development. Current business leaders must overcome a potential shortage with robust leadership development programs. And they must do that quickly. Likewise, new leaders must understand that an important part of their responsibilities includes developing new leaders. That may be difficult considering the big difference in the generations, but it must be done. The best way to develop good leaders for the future is to start early. Leadership training must begin when employees are first appointed to a managerial position.

Leaders must also continually adapt to changes in technology. As I've mentioned throughout this book, technology is the one fact that will continue to evolve. Not only is technology constantly changing, but how humans interact is changing as well. While the Millennial Generation is the most computer literate and high-tech capable of any, their children are the first generation truly born into the computer age. Children are using computers at a very young age with computers and other technologies becoming more and more central in early education.[2] That means that by the time this new generation enters the workplace, they will be techno-literate beyond anything seen before.

While I have restricted these pages to the study of generations in the United States, I don't think that will be necessary or wise in studies of future generations. After World War II, many formerly industrial and economically powerful nations were devastated. While America quickly switched from a wartime to peacetime economy and became very prosperous, other nations had to first recover from the effects of the war. As a result, what we might call a global Baby Boom Generation was very different between the U.S. and other nations. While that generation in the U.S. grew up in relative prosperity, people of the same age in much of the rest of the world were more focused on survival as their parents worked to rebuild their homelands. With the passage of time, that gap has been closed in most parts of the world and, especially with the internet allowing instant and global communication, the next generation will have a much more international and congruous nature. Though perhaps it's an overused cliché, it's true that the world has become a smaller place and where companies used to think nationally, they must now think globally. There are many organizations for which success will only come with at least some interaction outside the nation's borders. Another factor is immigration which, while by no means a new phenomenon, has taken on a new importance. Previous waves of immigrants often adopted American culture over the culture of their home country, but today's immigrants are more likely to integrate both cultures, fundamentally changing the dynamic in the U.S. and bringing the larger world to us. As a group, Millennials are probably more prepared for this shift than any other generation. While other generations have wrestled with race and gender issues in the workplace, Millennials pretty much expect these to be non-issues and they embrace all-comers. We will reach a point with the next generation where this won't even be a point of discussion.

If this all seems too much for a Boomer or Xer leader to handle, don't despair. The basics of leadership do not need to change. Leaders who follow these basics will continue to be successful, while those who don't will continue to have difficulties. It may seem a daunting task bringing three and sometimes four generations together to accomplish something good for the organization, but there are some specific things to remember that will make the job easier.

1. Everyone can be identified, numerically, with a specific generation. That identification can help define them but can also be the most dangerous thing a leader can know. Not every Boomer is, or was, a hippie and not every Xer is lazy and unmotivated. Quite the opposite is true. In fact both characterizations are the minority for that generation. While it is useful to understand the events that shaped a person's life, a leader must still evaluate each person as an individual.

2. Probably more than any time in the last century, the workplace has changed; fundamentally and irreversibly. That change has been facilitated by several influences. One is younger generations that are, in many ways, themselves fundamentally different. Another is the meteoric rise in technological capability that has created abilities only dreamed of a mere 30 or even 20 years ago and has fundamentally changed the youngest generation,

causing their brains to develop and function differently. No they can't really multi-task, but they can process information and switch between tasks extremely quickly.

3. No matter what generation a person comes from there are a few things that seem to be constant. Everyone wants to be respected. Everyone wants to know that their contribution is important and appreciated. Everyone wants to be on a winning team.

4. Leaders who don't recognize the abilities of their people will fail. In the past, a leader could continue to be an incompetent manager and leader and still succeed. The willingness of the new generations to speak out, and the global availability of the internet, serve to put those incompetent leaders on notice that they will no longer be able to hide behind the office door.

With that information in mind, there are some things that the individual generations can do to ease tension, improve the working environment, and perhaps prepare for success with the next generation.

It may seem odd to lump the Silent and Baby Boom Generations together as they were quite different; however, to Xers and Millennials, they tend to look similar. These two generations can rightfully be proud of what they've accomplished. They ushered the country through some very prosperous times and oversaw tremendous change. These generations still have much to offer. Unfortunately, it often seems to them that no one is particularly interested in their experience. Though it may sometimes seem to them that the world is moving too fast, that's the world we live in. It does move faster, but it's also full of exciting new opportunities. It falls to these generations to continue their efforts to teach and develop, but they must also be open to learn. Xers and Millennials see things that previous generations didn't and they are often not willing to accept the "we've always done it that way" answer. That's good because they often point out things to which those previous generations have become accustomed. They are leading the change that continues what the Boomers intended to do before they became the establishment.

As these two generations begin to hand over the reins to Xers and Millennials, the Boomer and Silent Generations must embrace change and celebrate the younger generation's achievements. Xers and Millennials will enjoy success beyond earlier generation's wildest dreams. At the same time, remember that a leader's responsibility is to train and develop leaders for the future. With Xers, that hasn't always gone well and many have not been sufficiently prepared for their leadership roles. In fact, Xers are in a perfect position to bridge the gap between Boomers and Millennials, as they tend to have a foot in each of those generations.

At the same time the Millennial Generation has burst on the scene, and like Boomers, their numbers are overwhelming. They also come to the workplace eager to succeed, but often without some of the basic skills their elders expect. Willingness to help newer workers adapt is a great quality, yet that need to adapt goes both ways. Xers and Millennials have much to offer; listen to them and don't judge them too quickly or harshly.

For Generation X. You stand in the middle. Many of you had a completely different childhood and young adult period than the generations before or after. Much of your generation feels the world is either ignoring you or is at least not willing to recognize what you have to offer. In many cases, that assessment is probably correct and it provides you with a hurdle that other generations did not experience. Though you may feel Boomers are an impediment to progress, think of them as runners in a race. They have been running as hard as they can, with a laser like focus on the finish line. They have been competing against a very large number of other runners and they don't appreciate anyone starting late in the race. Just as Boomers need to be tolerant, it's important for Xers to demonstrate the same tolerance. Your generation tends to have a different and somewhat jaded view of the world, and that can be healthy, but it can also be irritating to both Boomers and Millennials. Just as Boomers must make an effort to understand where you come from and what drives your opinions and attitudes, you must also understand that they have worked hard to get where they are and find today's rapid pace of change a little difficult to handle at times. A soft approach can be helpful.

For the Millennial Generation. Face it, you're different and frankly, in some ways you scare your elders in the workplace. You process information faster than previous generations and have a level of comfort with technology that other generations can only wish for. Your enthusiasm for using technology is taking American commerce to new levels. But, many members of older generations are concerned with your ability to communicate and your reputation for expecting the world to bend to your wishes. Overall, your enthusiasm for improvement and upgrade is appreciated, but it must be tempered with a desire to learn and an understanding that Boomers and many Xers have trouble keeping up with your pace.

What does the future hold? Leaders should be assured of one thing. Change! If anything, change will just continue to come faster and leaders must be able to adapt. They must develop the ability to sort good change from bad change, recognizing which is which and embracing the former while redirecting the latter. "We've always done it that way" is no longer an acceptable answer.

Whatever the point in time that is chosen to represent the beginning of the next generation, those people won't enter the workplace for some time. Leaders should be assured that they too will be different and bring new challenges, and more importantly, new opportunities. While Millennials are often credited with being the first completely connected generation, most didn't start that way. The next generation will be almost literally born with a cell phone in their hand!

It is evident that Silent and Boomer Generation leaders were not ready for the Xer and Millennial Generations. These two generations brought a level and pace of change that previous generations had not experienced and in many cases they just weren't prepared for that change. Xer and Millennial leaders may be better equipped to handle change brought by the next generation, but they must acknowledge that change will continue to come rapidly.

To be successful into the future, organizations of all types and sizes must work hard to keep their employees engaged by providing continual opportunities for development. While Boomers often were concerned with the corner office, titles, and compensation packages, that won't be sufficient in the future workplace. What are more attractive to young workers are opportunities for personal development and broader experiences. Yes, compensation will continue to be important, but how compensation is delivered will continue to change as more people seek opportunities for greater control.

Though it is dangerous to predict the future, I do believe that there will be a fairly significant change in the Millennial Generation. Whatever the +future holds, there will continue to be new generations interacting with older generations. That will bring conflict and require a high level of flexibility and understanding. Future generations will be successful when they understand their responsibility to learn from each other.

There is a Chinese proverb that says, "If you want happiness for a lifetime, help the next generation." That seems perfect advice for a leader with four generations in the workplace, and one on the way.

# Appendix A – The Timeline of Generations

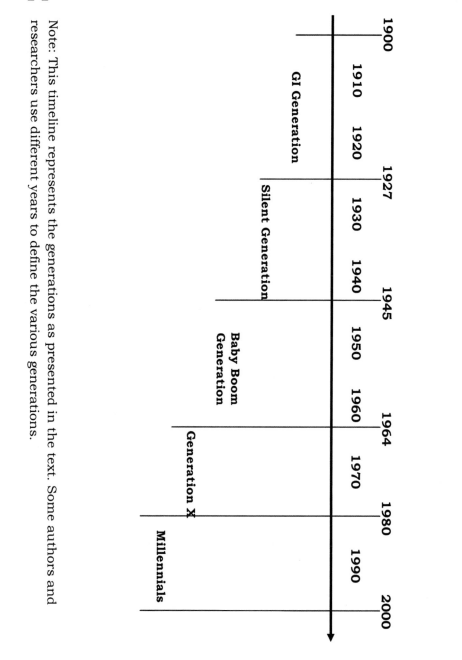

Note: This timeline represents the generations as presented in the text. Some authors and researchers use different years to define the various generations.

# Appendix B – Brief Facts About the Generations

GI Generation
- Boom (Roaring 20's)
- Bust (Great Depression)
- War (WW II and Korean War)
- Saw the automobile, airplane, penicillin, radio, television, space flight
- First time for large numbers of women in industrial jobs
- Group joiners - AARP, American Legion, Veterans of Foreign Wars, etc
- Seven U.S. Presidents

Silent Generation
- Significantly affected by the Depression
- Too young to serve in WWII but old enough for the Korean War
- First humans to walk on the moon – Armstrong and Aldrin
- Social leaders such as Martin Luther King and Cesar Chavez
- Counter-culture leaders such as Abbie Hoffman, Jane Fonda

Baby Boom Generation
- 78 Million babies born between 1945 and 1964
- New mobility – U.S. population center moved from western Indiana to Western Illinois
- Most educated generation up to this time

- Protest for such social issues – often led by Silent Generation members
- First big impact of T.V. – race issues and Vietnam War
- Woodstock
- Vietnam War
- Big four computer icons – Jobs, Wozniak, Gates, Allen
- Very high divorce rate
- Generally competitive in the workplace

Generation X
- Small Generation – 37 million
- Relatively stable economic conditions in early and young adult years
- Savings and Loan and Enron scandals and "dot com" collapse
- War in the Middle East
- Often the product of broken homes
- Pushed the limits and expanded technology
- Most educated generation – surpassed the Boomers
- Often hold a skeptical view of the world
- Not as likely to work long hours and weekends, but may take work home

Millennials
- Largest generation – 81 million
- Birth mothers from three generations
- Digital Natives
- Processes information more quickly than their parents
- Grew up with video games
- Leverages technology in new ways – relies heavily on the internet
- Wants technology in the workplace

- Generally very close to parents
- Often communicates in ways foreign to earlier generation, such as text messaging
- Always looking for ways to work more efficiently – willing to challenge the status quo
- Much more likely to quit a job and move on

# Notes

**Introduction**

[1] Jeylan T. Mortimer, and Michael J. Shanahan, eds., *Handbook of the Life Course* (New York: Springer Science and Media LLC, 2004) 9.

[2] "The 400," *Forbes* Special Issue, Oct 19, 2009.

**Chapter 1**
**Defining the Generations**

[1] Erick Erickson Learning Plane OnLine, "The Developmental Stages of Erik Erikson," http://www.learningplaceonline.com/stages/organize/Erikson.htm .

[2] Ibid

[3] Ibid

[4] Ibid

[5] Ibid

[6] Ibid

[7] Ibid

[8] Jeylan T. Mortimer, and Michael J. Shanahan , eds., *Handbook of the Life Course,* 3

**Chapter 2**
**Depression, Wars, and Starting Over**

[1] Larry Schweikart and Michael Allen, *A Patriots History of the United States* (New York: Sentinel), 548-533

[2] Ibid, p 553.

3 Robert Van Giezen and Albert E. Schwenk, "Compensation From Before World War I Through The Great Depression," U.S. Bureau of Labor Statistics, http://www.bls.gov/opub/cwc/cm20030124ar03p1.htm
4 Congressional Research Service Report for Congress "American War and Military Operations Casualties: Lists and Statistics." May 14, 2008. http://fas.org/sgp/crs/natsec/RL32492.pdf.

5U.S. Census "Historical National Population Estimates, July 1, 1900 to July 1, 1999." http://www.census.gov/popest/archives/1990s/popclockest.txt.

6 U.S. Census "United States Summary from the 1940 Census." 23 http://www.webcitation.org/5iRBWc0kx.
7 U.S. Census "1940 Census." www.census.gov.
8 Emily Yellin, *Our Mothers at War: American Women at Home and at the Front in World War II* (New York: Free Press, 2004) 46.
9 Ibid, 66-70

10 Data for this chart is taken from each decade's decennial census. Some birth and death data is derived from reports published by the United States Public Health Service National Office of Vital Statistics. All sources may be found at www.census.gov and www. http://www.cdc.gov/nchs/data/vsus/vsrates1900_40.pdf. Reliable birth and death data for the decades 1900 through 1940 is unavailable or unreliable. Recording of birth data began in 1915 and included only a few states, from which national data was derived.

[11] William Strauss and Neil Howe, *Generations: The History of America's Future 1584 - 2069* (New York: Harper Perennial, 1992), 267.

[12] Ibid, 266 - 267.

[13] Ibid, 267.

[14]Susan B. Carter et al., ed., *Historical Statistics of the United States, Millennial Edition On-Line* (Cambridge University Press), 2006. Table Ae 507 - 513. http://faculty.winthrop.edu/eckbergd/Course_materials/marriage%20and%20divorce.pdf.

[15] Herman S. Wolk, "The 'New Look'," *Air Force Magazine On-Line* 86, no. 8 (August, 2008) http://www.airforce-magazine.com/MagazineArchive/Pages/2003/August%202003/0803look.aspx.

[16] Data for this chart is taken from each decade's decennial census. Some birth and death data is derived from reports published by the United States Public Health Service National Office of Vital Statistics. All sources may be found at www.census.gov and www. http://www.cdc.gov/nchs/data/vsus/vsrates1900_40.pdf. Reliable birth and death data for the decades 1900 through 1940 is unavailable or unreliable. Recording of birth data began in 1915 and included only a few states, from which national data was derived.

[17] William Strauss and Neil Howe, *Generations: The History of America's Future 1584 - 2069,* 283

[18] History of the United Farm Workers and Cesar Chavez, http://www.ufw.org/_page.php?inc=research_history.html&menu=research.

[19] William Strauss and Neil Howe, *Generations: The History of America's Future 1584 - 2069*, 285 - 286.

[20]National Aeronautics and Space Administration, "Sputnik and the Dawn of the Space Age," Sputnik: The Fiftieth Anniversary," http://history.nasa.gov/sputnik/.

[21] Timothy Taylor, *America and the New Global Economy*, (Chantilly, VA: The Teaching Company), 4-5, 8

**Chapter 3**
**The Baby Boom Generation**

[22] "The Latest With Generation Jones," http://generationjones.com/2009latest.html.

[23] U.S. Census Bureau, "Statistical Abstract of the United States, 2003," 21-22.
As this is not intended as a scientific study of population figures, I have rounded the rates. The total birth and death numbers are derived from adding the actual census numbers and rounding down the total.

[24] Data for this chart is taken from each decade's decennial census. Some birth and death data is derived from reports published by the United States Public Health Service National Office of Vital Statistics. All sources may be found at www.census.gov and www. http://www.cdc.gov/nchs/data/vsus/vsrates1900_40.pdf. Reliable birth and death data for the decades 1900 through 1940 is unavailable or unreliable. Recording of birth data began

in 1915 and included only a few states, from which national data was derived.

[25] US Department of Labor, Bureau of Labor Statistics, "Household Data Annual Averages," p 194.

[26] U.S. Census Bureau, "Statistical Abstract of the United States, 2003," 20

[27] U.S. Census Bureau, "A Half-Century of Learning: Historical Statistics on Educational Attainment in the United States, 1940 to 2000," Table 1and Table 2. http://www.census.gov/population/www/socdemo/education/phct41.html.
The table does not include an entry for 1989 so I have used the number for 1990. Other tables in this study indicate that the difference between the two years is not significant to this book.

[28] Jack Wienber, http://www.bartleby.com/73/1828.html.

[29] "The Brown Foundation, "Brown vs. The Board of Education. About the Case," http://brownvboard.org/summary/.

[30] African American Odyssey, "The Civil Rights Era," http://memory.loc.gov/ammem/aaohtml/exhibit/aopart9.html .

[31] The Civil Rights Movement: 1954 to 1963, "Supreme Court Decides Brown vs. Board," http://faculty.smu.edu/dsimon/Change-Civ%20Rts.html. (Extracted from David Halberstam, Chapter 28, *The Fifties*, New York: Ballantine Books, 1994).

[32] Walter Rucker and James Nathaniel Upton, *Encyclopedia of American Race Riots: Vol 1 A-M*, (Westport, CT: Greenwood Press), 138.
For an example of the TV coverage of police using dogs and fire hoses in Birmingham go to

http://www.youtube.com/watch?v=j9kT1yO4MGg&feature=geo search.

33 Documents from the Women's Liberation Movement, "Female Liberation: A Joint Statement by Six Female Liberation Groups in Chapel Hill and Durham, N.C.," Special Collections Library, Duke University, http://scriptorium.lib.duke.edu/wlm/statement/.

34 The numbers for women's employment are derived from the decennial census. The census reports are at such lengthy intervals, they each present data in a different way. For this study I divided the total number of employed women by the total employed population to obtain a percentage. The census reports may be obtained from www.census.gov by typing 19XX Census in the search box where XX is the desired decade.

35 The History Place, "The Vietnam War," http://www.historyplace.com/unitedstates/vietnam/index-1945.html.

36 The "falling dominos" comment comes from a news conference on April 7, 1954 at which President Eisenhower was asked by Robert Richards of Copley Press "Mr. President, would you mind commenting on the strategic importance of Indochina to the free world? I think there has been, across the country, some lack of understanding on just what it means to us. "The President's News Conference of April 7, 1954," *Public Papers of the Presidents of the United States: Dwight D. Eisenhower, 1954* (Washington, D. C.: U. S. Government Printing Office, 1960), 382-83. http://www.historytools.org/sources/domino.html

37 Guido H. Stempel, Professor of Journalism, Ohio University. Letter to the New York Times dated September 7, 1988.

38 Michael Lang with Holly George-Warren, *The Road to Woodstock From the Man Behind the Legendary Festival*, (New York: Ecco, 2009).

[39] Ibid, 238

[40] Larry Schweikart and Michael Allen, *A Patriots History of the United States* (New York: Sentinel), 704.

[41] Timothy Taylor, *America and the New Global Economy*, (Chantilly, VA: The Teaching Company), 9.

[42] Ibid, pp 8 - 9

[43] U.S. Census Bureau, "Statistical Abstract of the United States, 2003), 72. To be fair, Generation X reached child-bearing years, generally considered to be women aged 18 - 34, in 1983 and so some of the increase may have been the result of that influence. However, the birth rate among those 20 years and younger was fairly low during this period.

[44] Harry S. Farber, "Is the Company Man an Anachronism? Trends in Long-Term Employment in the U.S, 1973 - 2006," (Working Paper #518, Princeton University, Industrial Relations Section, September 11, 2007).

[45] Dane Stangler, "The Coming Entrepreneurship Boom," (Ewing Marion Kaufman Foundation, June 2009), 4

[46] "Older Workers, Hit by Recession, Delay Retirement," ABC 7 News, Arlington, VA, February 20, 2009.

[47] Steve Hendrix, "Baby Boomers Find Growing Acceptance of Pot Smoking," *Washington Post*, Published in *The Albuquerque Journal*, November 22, 2009.

[48] Jonathan Pontell, "Stuck in the Middle," *USA Today*, January 27, 2009, Op-Ed, http://blogs.usatoday.com/oped/2009/01/stuck-in-the-mi.html.

[49] U.S. Bureau of Labor Statistics, "Current Population Survey," Table 9, http://www.bls.gov/cps/cpsaat1.pdf.

[50] U.S. Bureau of Labor Statistics, "The Employment Situation, September 2009," New Release, October 2, 2009

51 "Election Results 2008," *New York Times*, November 5, 2008, http://elections.nytimes.com/2008/results/president/exit-polls.html.
Numbers are derived from exit polls and telephone interviews conducted by Edison Media Research/Mitofsky International.
52 "Election Results," Edison Media Research/Mitofsky International, http://www.cnn.com/ELECTION/2004/pages/results/states/US/P/00/epolls.0.html.
53 Jonathan Pontell, "Stuck in the Middle," *USA Today*, January 27, 2009, Op-Ed, http://blogs.usatoday.com/oped/2009/01/stuck-in-the-mi.html.
54 Maureen Farrell, "America's Most Promising Companies," *Forbes*, October 5, 2009.

55 U.S. Census Bureau, Rose M. Kreider and Jason M. Fields, "Number, Timing, and Duration of Marriage and Divorces: 1996," 3, http://www.census.gov/prod/2002pubs/p70-80.pdf.

**Chapter 4**
**Generation X and the Millennials**

1 Sharon Jayson, "Parents, Kids Today More In Harmony," *USA Today*, August 12, 2009, 1D, http://rpproxy.iii.com:9797/MuseSessionID=59d1a1a6386b2b3ef08691be42fcbd9/MuseHost=galenet.galegroup.com/MusePath/servlet/BioRC?vrsn=149&locID=apl&srchtp=advanced&c=15&ste=28&tbst=asrch&tab=8&n=40&AS1=millennials&AI1=FA&docNum=CJ205686660&bConts=11.
2 U.S. Census Bureau, "Statistical Abstract of the United States, 2003," 72.

[3] Data for this chart is taken from each decade's decennial census. Some birth and death data is derived from reports published by the United States Public Health Service National Office of Vital Statistics. All sources may be found at www.census.gov and www. http://www.cdc.gov/nchs/data/vsus/vsrates1900_40.pdf. Reliable birth and death data for the decades 1900 through 1940 is unavailable or unreliable. Recording of birth data began in 1915 and included only a few states, from which national data was derived.

[4] Bruce Tulgan, *Managing Generation X: How to Bring Out the Best in Young Talent*, (New York: W.W. Norton & Co., 200) 41 - 51.

[5] "Moore's Law Made Real by Intel Innovation," Intel, http://www.intel.com/technology/mooreslaw/.

[6] Mark J.P. Wolf, *The Video Game Explosion: A History From Pong to Playstation and Beyond*, (Westport, CT, Glenwood Press, 2008) 29.

[7] U.S. Census Bureau, "Census Questionnaire Content, 1990 CQC-13," 2, http://www.census.gov/apsd/cqc/cqc13.pdf.

[8] Harry S. Farber, "Is the Company Man an Anachronism? Trends in Long-Term Employment in the U.S., 1973 - 2006," (Working Paper #518, Princeton University Industrial Relations Section, September 11, 2007).

[9] Joe Markert. "The Changing Demographics in the Healthcare Workforce," (Webinar by Professor Joe Markert, Rutgers University, November 11, 2009)

[10] Michelle Conlin, "For Gen X it's Paradise Lost," *Business Week*, June 30, 2003,

---

http://www.businessweek.com/magazine/content/03_26/b38 39081_mz021.htm.

[11] Niall Ferguson, *The Ascent of Money: A Financial History of the World*, (New York, The Penquin Press, 2008), 254-258.

[12] Ibid, 168-173

[13] "Older Workers, Hit by Recession, Delay Retirement," ABC 7 News, Arlington, VA, February 20, 2009.

[14] Michelle Conlin, "For Gen X its Paradise Lost," *Business Week*, June 30, 2003, http://www.businessweek.com/magazine/content/03_26/b38 39081_mz021.htm.

[15] Centers for Disease Control, "Births: Final Data for 2005," (National Vital Statistics Report, Vol 56, Number 6, December 5, 2007) Table 1.

[16] Data for this chart is taken from each decade's decennial census. Some birth and death data is derived from reports published by the United States Public Health Service National Office of Vital Statistics. All sources may be found at www.census.gov and www. http://www.cdc.gov/nchs/data/vsus/vsrates1900_40.pdf. Reliable birth and death data for the decades 1900 through 1940 is unavailable or unreliable. Recording of birth data began in 1915 and included only a few states, from which national data was derived.

[17] This chart is derived from both census and Center for Disease Control data. It should be noted that source data for 1960 and 1970 uses an initial age range of 15-19 while subsequent years use 18-19. This chart uses 18-19 since that is the numbers used for the years of interest. Data sources can be found at the following locations.

1960 data, http://www.cdc.gov/nchs/data/vsus/nat60_1.pdf
1970 data,
http://www.cdc.gov/nchs/data/mvsr/supp/mv22_12sacc.pdf
1980 - 2000 data,
http://search.census.gov/search?q=births+final+data+1990&bt
nG.x=0&btnG.y=0&btnG=Go&Submit.x=0&Submit.y=0&entqr=
0&ud=1&output=xml_no_dtd&oe=UTF-8&ie=UTF-
8&client=default_frontend&proxystylesheet=default_frontend&s
ort=date%3AD%3AL%3Ad1&site=census

[18] Lynn Silipigni Connaway, "Make Room for the Millennials,"
*Next Space, the OCLC Newsletter*, No. 10, (October 2008),
http://www.oclc.org/nextspace/010/research.htm.
[19] Marc Prensky, "Digital Natives, Digital Immigrants, Part 1" *On
the Horizon*, MCB University Press, 9 No. 5, (October 2001), 1-2,
http://www.marcprensky.com/writing/Prensky%20-
%20Digital%20Natives,%20Digital%20Immigrants%20-
%20Part1.pdf.
[20] Victoria Shannon, "15 Years of Text Messages a 'Cultural
Phenomenon'," *New York Times*, December 5, 2007, Technology
Section. On-Line Edition,
http://www.nytimes.com/2007/12/05/technology/05iht-
sms.4.8603150.html?_r=1&pagewanted=all.
[21] InfoPlease, "Internet Timeline," Family Entertainment
Network, http://www.infoplease.com/ipa/A0193167.html

[22] Joshua Rubinstein and David Meyer, "Is Multitasking More
Efficient? Shifting Mental Gears Costs Time, Especially When
Shifting to Less Familiar Tasks," *APA On-Line*, (August 5, 2001),
http://www.apa.org/releases/multitasking.html.

## Chapter 5
## Gender Issues and Women in the Workplace

[1] Data taken from Decennial Census available at
www.census.gov. Note that employment statistics counted the
workforce as all those over the age of 14 until the 1980 census
when the age became 15.

[2] Aparna Mitra, "Access to Supervisory Jobs and the Gender
Wage Gap Among Professionals," *Journal of Economic Issues*,
(December 2003), Posted on BNet,
http://findarticles.com/p/articles/mi_qa5437/is_4_37/ai_n29
053283/?tag=content;col1.

[3] U.S. Department of Labor, Bureau of Labor Statistics,
"Highlights of Women's Earnings in 2008," (July 2009)

[4] Catalyst Research, "Women in U.S. Information", Pyramids,
http://www.catalyst.org/publication/157/women-in-us-
information, January 2010. Note: In 2009, Catalyst instituted a
methodology change that makes comparison to previous annual
Corporate Officer statistics inappropriate.

[5] National Association of Women Business Owners, "WBO
Statistics," http://nawbo.org/section_103.cfm.

[6] James T. Bond, et.al., "Highlights of the National Study of the
Changing Workforce," Family and Work Institute, No 3, 2002, 4.
This survey was accomplished by telephone and was limited to
people 18 years or older who worked at a paid job or operated
an income producing business, were in the civilian labor force,
lived in the contiguous 48 states, and lived in a household with
a telephone. In households with more than one eligible person,
one was chosen at random. Participants received a $25 cash
honorarium as an incentive for participating.

[7] Ibid. 5.

[8] Ibid, 5.

[9] U.S. Census Bureau, "Statistical Abstract of the United States, 2003, 9

[10] Ibid, 11.

[11] U.S. Department of Labor, "Labor Force Characteristics by Race and Ethnicity, 2007," (September, 2008)

[12] Timothy Taylor, *America and the New Global Economy*, (Chantilly, VA: The Teaching Company), 38

[13] Ibid, 45.

[14] Ibid, 57 - 63.

[15] Bureau of Labor Statistics, "Labor Force Characteristics by Race and Ethnicity," (Report 1005, September, 2008), 1.

[16] Timothy Taylor, *America and the New Global Economy*, (Chantilly, VA: The Teaching Company),  43.

[17] Bureau of Labor Statistics, "Labor Force Characteristics by Race and Ethnicity," 2.

[18] The U.S. Census Bureau includes India, Afghanistan, Pakistan, and the Middle Eastern countries in the statistics for Asian immigration.

[19] Bureau of Labor Statistics, "Labor Force Characteristics by Race and Ethnicity," 2007, 1.

[20] Joe Markert. "The Changing Demographics in the Healthcare Workforce," (Webinar by Professor, Rutgers University, November 11, 2009)

**Chapter 6**
**But That Isn't Me!**
**Those Who Don't Fit**

[1] There certainly could be more study of the effect of family and surroundings on development within the generations; however, the outcome for leaders would be the same: people are individuals.

---

[2] Though often repeated, this quote is believed to have originated with Paul Kantner, a founding member of the rock band Jefferson Airplane.

[3] Michael Lang with Holly George-Warren, *The Road to Woodstock From the Man Behind the Legendary Festival*, (New York: Ecco, 2009), 166 - 167.

[4] Marc Prensky, "Digital Natives, Digital Immigrants, Part 2" *On the Horizon*, MCB University Press, 9 No. 5, (December, 2001), 3. http://www.marcprensky.com/writing/Prensky%20-%20Digital%20Natives,%20Digital%20Immigrants%20-%20Part2.pdf.

[5] Lynne C. Lancaster and David Stillman, *When Generations Collide: Who they Are. Why They Clash. How to Solve the Generational Puzzle at Work*, (New York: HarperCollins, 2002), 36 - 41.

## Chapter 7
## Leading the Generations

[1] This is a generalization. Many of the "management gurus" are still active and they have produced very progressive work that addresses issues brought about by multiple generations. However, many early "gurus" such as Maslow and Herzberg are no longer with us to modify and update their theories. Those theories are no less valuable, but must be adapted to our modern situations.

## Chapter 8
## What You Want is Not What I Need

[1]"Maslow's Hierarchy of Needs," Project Management Course, http://www.abraham-maslow.com/m_motivation/Hierarchy_of_Needs.asp.
[2] Ceylan Cizmeli, "Psychology in Business Management: Abraham Maslow's Eupsychian Management," http://www.psychology.sunysb.edu/ewaters/345/2007_maslow/maslow%20on%20management.pdf.

[3] Matt Richtel, "Providing Cell Phones for the Poor," *New York Times*, June 14, 2009, Technology Section. On-line http://www.nytimes.com/2009/06/15/technology/15cell.html This program was actually begun in the 1980s to provide landline phones to the poor for emergencies.

[4] Robert Putnam, *Bowling Alone: The Collapse and Revival of American Community,* (NY, NY, Simon and Schuster, 2000) For a detailed look at Putnam's data, go to http://www.bowlingalone.com/data.htm.

## Chapter 9
## How Do I Motivate Thee?
## Let Me Discover The Ways

[1] Fredrick Herzberg, et.al., *The Motivation to Work,* (New Brunswick, NJ, Transaction Publishers, 2004) 13 - 16
[2] Ibid, 15
[3] Joe Markert. "The Changing Demographics in the Healthcare Workforce," (Webinar by Professor, Rutgers University, November 11, 2009)

## Chapter 10
## I Know You Heard What You Think I Said
## But Did I Say What You Think You Heard?

[1] "Capitalizing on Effective Communication, How Courage, Innovation and Discipline Drive Business Results in Challenging Times," (Towers Watson, 2010), 10-13. This study involved 328 organizations representing 22 different industries (plus an "other" category). Organization size varied from under 1,000 members to over 25,000, but the study was heavily weighted towards the under 1000 category (35.2%). Though the study was international in scope, 43% of respondents were in the U.S. I extracted data for U.S. organizations only.

[2] "Capitalizing on Effective Communication, How Courage, Innovation and Discipline Drive Business Results in Challenging Times," 1-9.

## Chapter 11
## It Takes All Kinds
## Generations and Diversity in the Workplace

[1] "Most Americans Approve of Interracial Dating", Jeffery M. Jones. Gallup News Service, Oct 7, 2005. Available at http://www.gallup.com/poll/19033/Most-Americans-Approve-Interracial-Dating.aspx. Note that the survey only polled opinions based on white and black races.

[2] "Facing Age Discrimination as Young as 40", Abby M. Locke, August 26, 2010. Available at http://ops.theladders.com/career-advice/facing-age-discrimination-40?et_id=1446376819&sign=y&link_id=536

[3] Huntley Manhertz Jr., Ph.D., "The Generational Divide: Crucial Consideration or Trivial Hype?" (paper published by AchieveGlobal Inc, 2009) This study was compiled from the responses of 512 employees surveyed and was international in scope. Dr. Manhertz specifically mentions differences in eastern and western cultures but there does not appear to be a difference in the results from those surveyed from western cultures so I have included it here even though I have chosen not to use other studies with similar international flavor but which did not disseminate the results sufficiently to allow me to determine that the results were applicable to the more narrow focus of this book.

**Chapter 12**
**Why Should I Change?**
**Why Can't You Change?**

[1] Though there isn't much, there is a little. Strauss and Howe present a fairly balanced view of multiple generations as do Lancaster and Stillman.

[2] For a good analysis of this subject, see Neil Howe and William Strauss, "Helicopter Parents in the Workplace," *New Paradigm*, (November, 2002), http://www.wikinomics.com/blog/uploads/helicopter-parents-in-the-workplace.pdf.

[3] "LexisNexis Technology Gap Survey," World One Research. (March, 2009), http://www.lexisnexis.com/media/pdfs/LexisNexis-Technology-Gap-Survey-4-09.pdf, 26

[4] Ibid, 43

---

5 "How Young People View Their Lives, Futures and Politics: A Portrait of "Generation Next," The Pew Research Center For The People & The Press, January 2007, 15.
The Pew survey interviewed 1,501 adults ages 18 and older by telephone. To compensate for toll charges, cell phone respondents were offered an incentive of $10 for completing the survey. Pew reports that the sampling error was plus or minus 3.5 percentage points at 95% confidence.
6 "Building a Leadership Legacy," Gilberg Leadership Institute, 2006, 2-3.

## Chapter 13
## How Do I Keep Them From Leaving?

1 "American Workers Are Happy With Their Jobs and Their Bosses," Kelly Global Workforce Index, 2006.
http://www.kellyservices.com/res/content/global/services/en/docs/gws.pdf.
2 Job Opening and Labor Turnover Survey, United States Bureau of Labor Statistics, http://www.bls.gov/jlt/ (Users should access the database, then enter the parameters for "quit rate.")
3 Joe Markert. "The Changing Demographics in the Healthcare Workforce," (Webinar by Professor Joe Markert, Rutgers University, November 11, 2009)
4 Deal, J. *Retiring the generation gap: How employees young and old can find common ground.* (San Francisco, CA: Jossey-Bass/The Center for Creative Leadership). Cited by Jason Dobbs et. al., in "The Multi-Generational Workplace," (The Center on Aging and Workplace Flexibility, Boston College, July 2007), 1.

[5] Petula Dvorak, "Fairy Tale of Telecommuting is, Well, Just That," The *Washington Post*. Published in *The Albuquerque Journal,* January 10, 2010. This is an amusing account of one persons attempt to telecommute but also contains the results of research by the University of Connecticut's School of Business.
[6] "Managing Tomorrow's People: Millennials at Work: Perspective of a New Generation," Price Waterhouse Coopers, 2008. The majority of respondents to the survey were recent graduates who had been hired by Price Waterhouse Coopers. The survey was international in scope but the results cited here are strictly for U.S. respondents.
[7] "How Young People View Their Lives, Futures and Politics: A Protrait of "Generation Next," The Pew Research Center For The People & The Press, January 2007, 5, 12.
[8] Huntley Manhertz Jr., PhD, "The Generational Divide: Crucial Consideration or Trivial Hype?" 4-5.

## Chapter 14
## What Does The Future Hold And
## What Can I Do About It?

[1] This data comes from two different sources. Data for the years 2000 – 2007 can be found in the U.S. Census Bureau Statistical Abstract of the United States: 2011, Page 65, Table 78, available at http://www.census.gov/compendia/statab/2011/tables/11s0078.pdf. Data for 2008 and 2009 is taken from Provisional Data From the National Vital Statistics System, Nation Center for Health Statistics, CDC, available at http://www.cdc.gov/nchs/data/nvsr/nvsr59/nvsr59_03.pdf. This data is provisional and cannot be confirmed until the U.S. Census Bureau releases data from the 2010 census.
[2] Anya Kamanetz, "'A' is for App", *Fast Company*, April 2010.67 – 77.

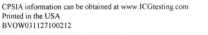

CPSIA information can be obtained at www.ICGtesting.com
Printed in the USA
BVOW031127100212

282598BV00006B/29/P